Luxor Lexicon

The A-Z Guide to Luxor

Connie Tindale

Edited by
Stan Kurowski and Christian Miller

All proceeds from the sale of this book are donated to Little Stars - Luxor Children's Trust for the benefit of Luxor's disadvantaged children.

Amun Publishing

Previous Publications

A Path through the Japanese Garden
Bonsai – A Guide to Successful Care and Creation
Turn Dreams into Reality
Your Time to shine.

Disclaimer
This book is meant to be an educational guide and all the material contained in the book is provided for information purposes only. No responsibility can be taken for any results or outcomes resulting from the use of this material. While every attempt has been made to provide information that is both accurate and effective, the author does not assume any responsibility for the accuracy or use/misuse of this information.

Cover designed by Stan Kurowski
Typeface Garamond size 11 points

Published by: Amun Publishing, Monongahela, Grove Road, Hethersett, Norfolk. NR9 3JP United Kingdom

ISBN-978-0-9574000-1-6

Contents

Introduction

This Lexicon is not meant to be a conventional Guide to Luxor listing hotels and restaurants or a treatise on Egyptian history; it is simply an A-Z insight to the things I learned during fifteen years of living and working in this fascinating country. It is a personal view of Luxor but gives the information that I wish I had been able to read when I first came to live in Egypt with its big smiles, constant sunshine and bewildering culture.

In the present, Egypt is going through a time of transition but has a bright future as it moves forward into a fledgling democracy. One day Luxor will be the largest open-air museum in the world. In the past, Luxor was the centre of the world to those who lived in it but, as Egyptologists are notoriously argumentative over events that happened 3,000 years ago, all entries relating to Egyptology have been kept brief. A reading list has been provided for those who wish to study this subject more deeply.

Over the years I developed an intense love of Egypt and consider myself privileged to have met so many Egyptian people who taught me about their beliefs, religions and culture and allowed me to share their lives.

Connie Tindale
2013

Abu el Haggag Mosque

A

Abu – Aywa

Abu – (abou) - means 'father' so Abu el Haggag means 'father of Haggag'.

Abu el Haggag – is the man who brought Islam to Luxor in the 7th century and is revered as a Muslim saint. He is remembered through a Moulid which takes place annually, three weeks before the start of Ramadan. The Moulid parade goes from Luxor Temple and circles the town. Its floats emulate the Pharaonic Opet Festival as many take the shape of the boats that once brought Amun's statue from Karnak Temple to Luxor Temple where he would greet Mut his celestial wife. Abu el Haggag's body is buried in a shrine in the entrance room to the mosque, which was built on top of Luxor Temple. This mosque is the oldest in Luxor, and has recently been restored to show the tops of the columns in Luxor Temple below it. It is open to visitors but remember to observe tradition and remove your shoes when entering. Women should be respectful and cover their hair.

Abu el Haggag Square – is the name of the open-sided piazza that was created next to Luxor Temple in 2005/2006. It is used for recreation, demonstrations and public events and is a popular place for Egyptian families to picnic.

Abu Naaka – is Luxor's biggest kitchen shop and is situated in an alley off the Salah el Din end of Television Street commonly referred to as 'Plastic Street'. The owner can be found in the street area of the shop and is usually bad tempered and shouts a lot but his shop is stocked with a vast array of household items.

Abu Simbel – is not only an exquisite temple built by Ramses II, it is a superb example of engineering as the whole temple was moved stone by stone to save it from being drowned in Lake Nasser when the Aswan high dam was constructed. The temple is in a similar position as before but on higher ground and backed by a false 'mountain'. It can be reached by road or by air from Aswan. However as the journey is of some 300 km it can make a very long day if travelled by road. There are two temples on the site; one fronted by vast seated statues of Ramses himself and another dedicated to his wife Nefertari and the goddess Hathor.

Abydos – is the most important site in the cult of Osiris as, in mythology, this is where Isis is said to have located Osiris's head. The mortuary temple of Seti I, completed by Ramses II, is the most popular monument in this vast archaeological site and the reliefs that adorn its walls are second to none. There is an important relief depicting the names of the Pharaohs stretching back to the foundation of the unified country (the so-called 'Kings List'). The town is clean and quiet but you will have an armed guard with you if you venture out of the main temple to explore the very interesting areas behind it. The guards are not intrusive and are there for your protection. It takes about four hours to get there by car from Luxor and is well worth the effort especially as you can visit the Hathor Temple at Dendera on the way. You can also take the train from Luxor to El Balyana and then get a taxi from the station to Abydos which is about 10 km away - you are likely to have a police escort between the station and the temple. The Osirion is at the rear of the temple.

Abyia – an abyia is the long outer dress that Egyptian women wear when they leave the house. It is usually black and sometimes has a zip up the front so that it is easily removed. A gellabyia is worn beneath it.

ACE – (Animal Care in Egypt) is a veterinary charity offering free care for working animals in the Luxor area. It is managed by Kim and is situated in a new building close to the Airport Road. It also offers treatment and boarding for small animals but this incurs a charge as it is outside their charitable remit.

Adoratrix– for several hundred years prior to the Greek invasion the Amun Adoratrices (high priestesses) wielded the wealth and power of Karnak Temple. The title of Divine Adoratrix 'God's wife of Amun' was originally only held by royal women who were given full pharaonic powers; ruling as Pharaohs in Upper Egypt, while their husbands/brothers ruled in Lower Egypt.

Later the title was also granted to lower born women. The 26th dynasty Adoratrix Nitocris is buried in a chapel at Medinet Habu along with her natural mother and adopted grandmother.

Afrit – is a malevolent ghost with demonic powers. There is still a strong belief on the west bank that 'afrits' infest the tombs of the Valley of the Kings at night.

Afterlife – the ancient Egyptians' obsession with getting into the Afterlife created work for thousands of people in Luxor (Thebes) and led to the creation of the magnificent temples and tombs. Entering the Afterlife was not a once and only thing; the process had to be repeated daily for eternity. The instructions for getting into the Afterlife were given in the funerary texts of the Book of the Dead and the Book of the Gates. At first it was believed that only the king could get into the Afterlife but that was later extended to include those who had royal favour. By the New Kingdom era, the weighing of the heart ceremony was added and that allowed all good people to become eternal. The whole process was designed to reunite the Ka which left the body on death, to the Ba which remained with it. For eternal life to be gained, the Ba had to be released so that the Ka and the Ba could fly away from the tomb together each day with the Ba returning to the body again each night. Mummification was designed to preserve the body from decay so that it could be used on this daily journey.

Afwan – simply means 'that's OK', 'you are welcome' or words to that effect. It will often be said to you when you thank someone or even when you say 'no' to someone who wants to sell you something. It is a polite acceptance of the situation.

Age – you may find people asking you how old you are. ('Cam senna – how many years'). In hot climates people have a tendency to age rapidly and you will be asked out of curiosity not out of rudeness and people will usually assume that you are a lot younger than you actually are. The age of majority in Egypt for both men and women is 21 years.

Agilla – is Arabic for bicycle and is a common form of transport in Luxor – usually with their riders ignoring all traffic laws. You can hire bicycles on both sides of the river.

Agriculture – Only 5% of Egypt's vast area of land can sustain life and that 5% is in the Delta and a narrow strip that follows the Nile, so agricultural land is at a premium but is constantly being eroded by illegal building. Originally the annual flood of the Nile dictated where things would grow but now the land is irrigated by diesel-fuelled pumps drawing water from a network of canals. In Upper Egypt, the main crop appears to be sugar cane but maize and wheat are also grown along with a whole range of fruit and vegetables. Sugar cane is a swamp plant and needs huge amounts of water. This has affected the water table and unfortunately this has had a very negative effect on the stonework of the temples. Egypt is one of the world's biggest consumers of wheat and it used to be the breadbasket of North Africa but now it imports more wheat than it grows. Egypt is famed for its cotton but the plants do not thrive in Luxor's heat. Work is now being done to try and irrigate remoter desert areas with piped waste water.

Ahmose I – was the founder of the 18th dynasty. During his reign he revived trade and completed the expulsion of the Hyksos from the Delta region, re-establishing Theban rule over the whole of Egypt. His mummy is in Luxor Museum.

AIDS – there are cases of AIDS in Egypt although the country is apparently in denial about it. However, there are far fewer cases than in western countries. In 2010 there were 3,919 known cases (ACCAS Report) but few will admit to being infected so the figures will be grossly understated. UNAID estimate that there are about 9,500 people who are HIV positive and that 1,000 people have died of AIDS. They estimate that 1,500 women of 15 years and older are HIV positive which has unfortunately led to an increasing incidence of children being born with the condition. Condoms are not widely used in Egypt and many are of inferior quality so wives do not always have adequate protection from husbands who are bi-sexual or 'work the sex trade' and put themselves and their families at risk. There is still a great stigma about HIV and AIDS and the knowledge that someone has had a test is enough to get them ostracised so even those at risk are seldom tested. An AIDS test is mandatory for non-Egyptians seeking work permits.

Air-Conditioning – all the major hotels and many restaurants are air-conditioned ('takeef') and so are the newer taxis. However, there are frequent power cuts which can leave you sweltering and in some areas the power supply is so inadequate that it is impossible to run an air conditioner effectively. The better units have a built-in heating system which is of great use during the winter months when temperatures can plummet. Taxi drivers are notoriously reluctant to switch on the air-conditioning as it uses more benzene and will usually only open a window even when you are melting. If you question the driver about it then he may suddenly lose all ability to speak English and profess to not understand but saying 'Shaggar it takeef' ('turn on the air-con') to him may work and stop you flaking out with heat exhaustion.

Airport - Luxor International Airport is situated 7 km from town. It takes about 15 minutes for a taxi to get there from central Luxor and will cost around 50 LE plus any tip that you wish to give. Airport security is tight and only passengers are allowed beyond the barrier to check-in. All non-Egyptians have to complete an arrival or departure card when entering or leaving the country. In addition to international flights there are daily domestic flights to Cairo and Aswan and several flights each week to Hurghada and Sharm el Sheikh. On arrival in Luxor the customs officials can be rude and officious but have a tendency to allow first-time visitors to pass through without bothering them. (See International Airports).

Aish – is Arabic for bread and refers to all kinds of bread not just loaves. Egyptian bread has a tendency to be heavy due to the kind of flour used but is delicious when freshly cooked. Flat bread forms part of the staple diet and is heavily subsidised in government bakeries but is not always of good quality.

Akhenaten – was an 18th dynasty Pharaoh who was originally called Amenhotep IV but changed his name to Akhenaten when he stopped worshipping Amun and adopted Aten as the only god. He built a new city to Aten, called 'Akhetaten' (Horizon of the Aten), at a deserted place between Luxor and Cairo, (modern day Tel el Armana) but there is little of this now left. He was the husband of Nefertiti and is assumed to be the father of Tutankhamun but this has been cast into doubt following DNA analysis of a mummy that was found in KV55. This mysterious mummy is certainly the father of Tutankhamun and everyone thought that they had found the mummy of the heretic Pharaoh but then it was pointed out that the mummy (whoever it was) could not be the grandfather of the two foetuses found in Tutankhamun's tomb. As these foetuses had been assumed to be the offspring of Tutankhamun and his wife Ankhesenamun, the mystery continues. As this all happened more than 3,000 years ago, it is unlikely that a long lost relative is going to pop out of the woodwork and explain it all. His move towards monotheism was not successful as the people resumed worship of their old gods after his death.

Al Fatiha – is the opening verse of the Koran. It starts with 'Bismillah al-rahman al-raheem' (in the name of Allah, the most compassionate, the most merciful) and is widely used in prayer. It is broadcast from the minaret in the calls to prayer so you will hear it regularly five times each day.

Alabaster – comes in two forms and several colours but the type found in Luxor is of the calcite variety which is the hardest form but still soft enough to carve easily. It has a translucent lustre which makes it attractive for ornamental use and there are many alabaster workshops making lamps, bowls and ornaments on the west bank.

Alexander the Great – conquered Egypt (which was part of the Persian Empire) in 331 BCE. After Alexander's death in Mesopotamia in 323 BCE his body was kidnapped by his followers and brought to Egypt for burial. The journey took 4 years to complete. He was buried in Alexandria in a solid gold coffin which is thought to have been melted down to pay for

Alexandria's magnificent lighthouse. He carried on the tradition of building and had a shrine to himself constructed in the holiest part of Luxor temple, where you can see him portrayed as a Pharaoh.

Allah – is the Arabic name of the one and only God, revered by Muslims worldwide. According to the holy book of Islam (the Koran or Qur'an) there are 99 names (attributes) for Allah such as (1) 'al rahman' (the compassionate) (2) 'al raheem' (most merciful) through to (99) 'saboor' (the patient). At the beginning of a formal announcement on TV or elsewhere and at the beginning of many personal letters you will hear or see 'Bismillah al rahman al raheem' (in the name of Allah the most compassionate and most merciful.) Allah is the same God as worshipped by Copts and all other religions 'of the book'. The difference is only in a name.

Allahu Akbar – (God is great.) You will hear this at every prayer time in Luxor when it is broadcast from the mosque.

Alms – the giving of alms is one of the five pillars of Islam and is done discretely. You will often see Egyptians slip small notes into the palms of old and disabled people. Alms are collected from households annually by the mosques ('zakat') and are distributed amongst the poorest people in the area. This is not the same as tipping which is given for a service. Alms are given purely with a desire to help.

Ambulance – in Luxor, the emergency number to call an ambulance is 123.

Amenhotep III – (also known as Amenophis) was the 9th Pharaoh of the 18th dynasty whose images (the colossi of Memnon) are, at present, all that is left of his massive temple in the west bank necropolis. However, excavation work has been on-going there for the last two years and several more very large statues have been uncovered. Most of the temple's stones were taken and used elsewhere including the mortuary temple of Ramses II. This area is not yet open to the public. He was also responsible for the earlier parts of Luxor Temple primarily the colonnade, the sun court and further rooms to the south. He was buried in the Western Valley rather than the Valley of the Kings and his tomb is at present being restored but is also closed to the public.

Amon Hotel – is in the Gezera village area of the west bank and is only a short walk from the ferry. It is a pleasant hotel with a small but atmospheric garden and worth considering for a holiday stay.

Amulet – small carved figures that brought protection from the gods were commonly worn by ancient Egyptians. Examples are the Ankh, which is a symbol for life, and the Wedjet-Eye which wards off evil. Continued protection in the Afterlife was ensured by inserting amulets in mummy wrappings. Sometimes, hundreds of these were put in the layers of bindings. A favoured amulet was the scarab which was placed over the heart which was left in the body. Unfortunately, the possible presence of precious amulets led to mummies being hacked about by tomb robbers. These symbols are still worn as pendants by those who wish to wear something other than a cross or a St. Christopher and can be found in the jewellery shops and the souk. (See Scarabs, Ankh and Wedjet-Eye.)

Amun – 'the hidden one' was Luxor's principal god and is usually depicted with blue skin and sitting on a throne with a headdress of two large feathers. Luxor Temple, Karnak Temple and most of the mortuary temples are dedicated to him. He is part of a triad as father of Khonsu and husband of Mut. The priesthood of Amun was immensely powerful and at times had greater power than the Pharaoh. Amun can also be found on the temple walls in his guise as 'Amun-Min' with his flail and greatly exaggerated erect penis. Following the rise of Thebes as an administrative centre it became an Amun cult-centre and Amun was merged with the creator god Ra to become the all-powerful Amun-Ra.

Anger – Egyptian men are confrontational and argue with each other quite frequently. They stand face to face, shout and gesticulate but seldom come to blows and then quite suddenly the situation defuses and they walk away from each other as though nothing had occurred. (You are likely to find yourself getting angry over several things like the constant hassle and poor service, but getting angry only raises your blood pressure and does not change anything.)

Ankh – is the hieroglyph for life and takes the form of a cross with a looped top. It can be seen frequently in the temples and tombs being carried, usually in the right hand, by Pharaohs or gods. There are some exquisite reliefs in Medinet Habu of the gods pouring a series of ankhs over the head of the Pharaoh, in effect pouring life over him. It was a very powerful amulet and was inserted into mummy wrappings as well as being worn. Silver ankhs are still worn as pendants and can be bought in the souk.

Antibiotics – come in a variety of strengths and can be bought over the counter at any pharmacy. Ciprofloxacin, Antinal; Flagyl, Penicillin, Amoxicillin, etc. are all available. Self-medication is never really advised but in an emergency it can stop a problem becoming a catastrophe. If you get a chest infection, self-medication in Luxor is so high that it is likely to be resistant to the usual Amoxicillin treatment and you may have to resort to something stronger. If you start taking a course of antibiotics please take the whole course and not just a single dose as bugs are becoming increasingly resistant. However, a single dose of Flagyl is effective against giardia although the most common complaints are diarrhoea and chest infections against which Antinal and ciprofloxacin are respectively very effective.

Antinal – A local medicine for stomach upsets – it is more effective in Egypt than the European equivalents.

Antiques – you may be secretly offered antiques, particularly shabti figures. Do not buy them. If they are fakes then you will lose your money. If they are real then you could be asking to be arrested at the airport as you attempt to get them out of the country. You would then be imprisoned. Smuggling antiquities is a criminal offence. It is not worth the risk.

Ants – come in every conceivable size from tiny pin-head insects that swarm in huge numbers through to large ones that tramp along the floors and up the walls in single file but which you feel could carry off your suitcases instead of the sugar in the bowl. They are mostly harmless but the really small ones sting and can cause nasty lumps if you react to formic acid.

Anubis – is the jackal headed god who attends the weighing of the heart ceremony. He is the son of Osiris and his sister Nephthys. His skin is black, not to show the colour of the jackal but reminiscent of rotting flesh and the colour of Nile silt.

Apophis – is the Greek name for the ancient evil god Apep. He is the huge serpent that you see on the walls of many of Luxor's tombs. He is the embodiment of all evil and has immense length signifying his strength. Usually he is shown battling with Ra to stop the day beginning. However, the god Seth travels with Ra in his solar boat and overcomes Apep in this daily battle but this is not exactly a fight between good and evil as Seth himself is associated with evil but is more to emphasise the constant struggle that Ra has bringing the sun back each day.

Appliqué – there are some wonderful appliqué cushion covers and wall hangings in the souk. Some are of birds and animals but the intricate geometric Islamic designs are the most evocative of Egypt.

Apricots – ('mish mish') are grown in Egypt but are expensive in relative terms and considered a luxury item to such an extent that the term 'fil mish mish' meaning 'in apricots' has come to mean 'in your dreams'. Saying 'fil mish mish' to a trader or taxi driver who is quoting a ridiculously high price usually defuses the situation and brings about laughter.

Arab Spring – is the name given to the revolutionary wave of protests that swept across North Africa (including Egypt) at the end of 2010 and the beginning of 2011. This saw the overthrow of several dictatorships. North Africa is still in a transitional state but there is great hope for the future. Luxor was as affected by this as any other city in Egypt. Since then the ambience of Luxor has changed, its safety has been questioned and there has been a downturn in tourism but it will recover.

Arabeya – in Arabic any car or cart is called an 'arabeya' (even the street cleaners little carts) but is usually applied to the service cars that constantly circle the town. Once you get used to them they are a good way of getting about. A journey costs 50 piastras no matter where you get on or get off. However, with Egypt's present fuel shortages and the threat of the loss of fuel subsidies, this is likely to increase.

Arabic – is the national language of Egypt and all legal documents have to be in Arabic format. It is not an easy language to master as there are more than a dozen sounds that do not occur in the English language, many of which are made in the back of the throat. Arabic is read from right to left and there are no vowels in its written form. Vowel sounds are determined by the place of a letter in relation to other letters. Fortunately, many of the signs in Luxor are written in English as well as Arabic but this is not the case in non-tourist areas.

Arcane Egypt – ancient Egypt depended on its arcane (mysteries known only by a few) knowledge of the secrets and spells that governed all aspects of life and death. Despite its Muslim background, rural Egypt (Luxor) is still arcane and there is a great belief in the evil eye but now it is a west bank sheikh rather than a shaman who dispenses spells. Modern day Wicca and Alchemy are closely aligned to the old beliefs and Isis and Thoth remain respected pagan deities. Tourists still come to Luxor to worship at the feet of Amun and Egypt related Tarot cards are very popular.

Arkwright's Emporium – Can be found in St. Joseph Street and is noticeable from 'Granville's' bike parked outside. Its name refers to a British comedy series called 'Open all Hours'. The shop is a favourite among tourists as it sells sandwiches, cakes and packed lunches which are ideal for the day out on the river and is loved by expats who crave Digestive Biscuits and want big bags of Whiskas to feed their cats.

Armant - Armant is the ancient Greek settlement of Hermonthis, and is located about 12 miles south of Luxor. Armant thrived through the middle-kingdom eras and some large temples were built there in the 18th dynasty but these have now all gone. A temple to Montu still exists and there is a large Coptic monastery dedicated to St. George where there is an annual festival. There was also a temple to Cleopatra but the stones from this were used to build a 19th century sugar refinery. The small-gauge trains that you may see on the west bank loaded with sugar cane are heading there.

Armed Guards – you will notice that some of the non-uniformed guards at the temples wear jackets no matter how hot it is. Quite often, a sub-machine gun is lodged under the guard's arm and concealed inside his jacket but can often be seen as, for ease of access, the jackets are never buttoned. Do not let this alarm you as this is solely for your protection and has been standard practice since the massacre at the Hatshepsut Temple in 1997. There are armed guards on the night trains to and from Cairo but these are uniformed soldiers.

Artists – Luxor has always attracted accomplished artists. From the tomb paintings of ancient Egypt through to the atmospheric 19th century paintings of David Roberts, Luxor has been represented on scroll and canvas. Modern artists are equally as accomplished and their work can be found in the galleries that are spread around Luxor. David Roberts' prints are to be found in all the book shops.

Assasif – The Assasif tombs are close to Hatshepsut temple, and you get the ticket for them from the temple ticket office. The tombs you can visit are: Kheruef, 18th dynasty, with paintings of Amenhotep III and the young Amenhotep IV (Akhenaten); Ankhor, with scenes of beekeeping; and fishing; and the tomb of Pabasa. There is a lot of excavation work going on (2013) in the south Assasif and recently the remains of a mud brick pyramid were found there. The area is mainly of interest to Egyptologists rather than general tourists.

Assiut – lies several hours to the north of Luxor and is the main administrative centre for Upper Egypt. There is a large university there and a well-equipped hospital. If someone in Luxor is seriously ill or needs specialist treatment they are often sent to Assiut. Buses to Hurghada go there before proceeding to the Red Sea.

Aswan – lies to the south of Luxor and can be reached by road and rail. Aswan also has an International airport. The train journey takes about 4 hours from Luxor. It is an ancient garrison city which protected the southern borders of Egypt from the Nubians. The beautiful granite used in the obelisks and statues of the Pharaohs was quarried there. The temple of Isis at Philae is a superb example of Ptolemaic architecture and other places of interest are the Fatimid Cemetery, Nubian Museum, Aswan Museum, Kitchener and Elephantine Islands, the High Dam and the unfinished obelisk.

Aubergines – are grown locally and play a large part in the Egyptian diet. You can see many fields of them on the west bank which often have black kites circling, looking for rodent prey. Aubergines are used in many dishes and are delicious when cooked in batter. They are also the major ingredient in a delicious salad accompaniment called baba ganoush.

Avenue of Sphinxes – Luxor's Avenue of Sphinxes originally stretched the 3km distance from Karnak to Luxor Temple and was used in the annual Opet Festival. There were six shrine stations along the route with each serving a different purpose in the praise and comfort of Amun. Most of the Avenue was lost under the buildings of modern Luxor but some clearance has taken place and part of the Avenue has been restored. The Avenue was lined with sphinxes by Nectanebo (380-362 BCE) in the 30th dynasty and the lion body of each sphinx bears his head. A restored section of the avenue was enhanced with floodlighting in February 2013.

Awamia – is a village area of Luxor which lies at the southern end of the town around the Sheraton Hotel. Masses of illegal high-rise building is taking place there (2013) by people hoping to avoid building regulations while the government is in disarray. However, part of the area is being officially developed as the new municipal swimming pool and the Culture Palace are both situated there on the main road.

Aywa – is Arabic for 'yes'.

Hot Air Balloon Over Thoth Hill

B

Ba – Butane Gas

Ba – in ancient times, the Ba was considered as the force that made a person unique. It was not exactly the soul but something closer to being the essence of the person and their personality. Whereas the Ka (life spark) fled the body on death, the Ba persisted into the Afterlife. The Ba is shown in texts as a bird with a human head which flies out of the tomb to meet the Ka so that life could continue beyond the grave.

Baba Ganoush – is an Egyptian salad accompaniment made up of roasted aubergines, garlic, tahina and olive oil that is mashed into a thick paste. It is sometimes spiced with hot chillies that can catch you unaware.

Back Packing – Egypt is often one of the first or last stops on the itinerary of backpackers travelling the length of Africa. Luxor is a vital destination and there are budget hotels and campsites on both sides of the river: the Bob Marley House Hostel is off Television Street; and the Rezeiki Camp and Hostel is on the road to Karnak. The Kareem Hostel and the El Salaam Camp are on the west bank. The El Salaam camp is situated on the riverbank, about 2km from the ferry.

Bad-Eyes – rural Egyptians have a great belief in what they refer to as 'bad eyes' which stem usually from jealousy. Sometimes, they will go to great lengths to avert bad-eye problems. Male babies are greatly prized and it has been known for parents to dress their baby boy as a girl to avoid bad-eye jealousies. Bad-eye remedies can be obtained from the local sheikh.

Bag Snatching – unfortunately since the 'revolution' of the Arab Spring in January 2011, incidences of bag snatching have been on the increase. The method employed is for a motor bike to drive past slowly and for the pillion passenger to grab a bag and then roar off. This happens to Egyptian women as well as to tourists and is probably largely opportunistic. To counter the problem women should carry their bags with the strap across their body and keep the bag away from the road side of the pavement. Also they should only carry essential items. Passports, jewellery, travel documents and holiday money should stay safely back at the hotel. When you are in town you would only ever need a photocopy of your passport so it is safe to leave it behind.

Baksheesh – Baksheesh means 'gift' but its meaning has been corrupted to include tipping. Other than beggars, adults seldom approach you for baksheesh unless they have done a service of some kind and are expecting a tip but children often walk up to you with an open hand muttering 'baksheesh' or 'hello money' and can get more on their way to and from school than a working man earns. Please do not hand over money just because someone asks for it but be generous with your tips when they have been earned as Egypt is a very poor country and wages are low. A small offer of baksheesh in the temples may gain you access to areas apparently off-limits such as closed temples and roped off chapels. If nobody is around, baksheesh of 20 LE may be sufficient to persuade the guard to let you take photographs (usually prohibited) inside a tomb. Whether or not you take advantage of this is up to your own conscience.

Baladi – you may hear of baladi bread, baladi chickens and baladi salads. It just indicates that it is traditional and the kind of item found in most village homes.

Balloon Flights – there are several balloon companies in Luxor with a very wide price range and an even wider safety record. Taking a balloon flight can be a wonderful experience but check the insurance position of the company as it is unlikely to be covered by your tour company's insurance. Ask to see the insurance certificate as some companies have been known to lie blatantly about their insurance cover. Hod Hod Balloons can be recommended and although they have highest price they also have the best safety record so it worth the extra - flights are approximately £80.00 sterling but can be as low as £25.00 with some companies. Sadly there was a balloon accident in February 2013 where 19 people lost their lives when a balloon caught fire and a gas cylinder exploded. Accidents do happen but they are rare.

Bananas and Banana Island – ('moz') there are over 200 different types of bananas in cultivation and although not all of them grow on Banana Island which is close to the east bank, the plantation there is still impressive. It used to be open to the public but the license was lost a few years ago and the coffee shop there closed. There is a banana plantation open to visitors at Djorf on the west bank which is calling itself 'Banana Island' but it is actually on the river bank. Egyptian bananas are small but inexpensive and taste wonderful.

Bango – is the local name for hashish or marihuana. It is technically illegal but is widely available.

Banks – Banks are open from Sunday–Thursday with varying opening times but most seem to close around 3.00 pm. Banks close at lunchtime during Ramadan. All the major Egyptian banks have branches in Luxor and there are also branches of Barclays and HSBC. (See cash machines). Several are open in the evenings for currency exchange.

Banter – the banter used by shop-keepers to get you into their shops is fairly standard. The first thing usually asked is 'what country'. This is not asked out of interest but to assess financial status and propensity to bargain. The British are known to walk away rather than argue about price so outrageous first offers are usually toned down. Others may ask you for a translation of a word (which they already know the meaning of) in an attempt to get your attention.

Barbers – for an Egyptian, getting his hair cut is serious business and can take hours of trimming, snipping and grooming plus a shave and sometimes 'threading' which removes all the fine hairs from the face as well as the coarse ones. It turns into a social occasion. So, if you are calling in at the barber's shop make sure that you have plenty of time. Prices can range from 10 LE to 50 LE depending on how gullible the barber thinks you are and how generous you wish to be. Take care of any cuts you may receive as Egypt has the highest Hep C rate in the world.

Barques – are the boats of the gods and played an important role in many ancient Egyptian religious ceremonies so a barque of some kind was placed in every tomb. A solar barque was thought to carry Amun-Ra across the sky each day and through the Underworld each night. They were very important in Luxor as barques, borne on the shoulders of shaven-headed priests, were used during the Opet festival to carry statues of Amun, Mut and Khonsu from Karnak Temple to Luxor Temple.

Bats – fruit bats can be seen flying around both the town and the countryside at sunset. They are nocturnal, small compared with other fruit bats and harmless. They are only looking for food and feed mainly on dates.

Beer – the main beers sold in Luxor are Stella and Saqqara which is 10% stronger than Stella. You can expect to pay anything from 10 LE to 35+ LE for a can depending on where you are. Hotel prices can be extortionate. A nice place to have a cold beer and a bite to eat is Sindbad Coffee Shop near Luxor Temple. The waiters are polite and the beer reasonably priced but no alcohol is sold there during Ramadan. The widest range of beers (and wines) is sold in JJ's bar in Karnak where an excellent band performs regularly.

Bees – feature strongly in temple decorations. Deeply carved images of bees can clearly be seen on the columns of Karnak's hypostyle hall. Bee-keeping is shown in the wall paintings of several tombs and the products of honey ('asal') and wax were used extensively in ancient times. Modern day farmers still keep bees for honey production. It comes in dark and light forms that indicate from which flowers the bees gathered the pollen. The bee is the hieroglyph for 'bity' (King of Lower Egypt). (See Cartouche and Hieroglyphs.)

Beggars and Begging – wherever you are in the world you will find beggars. In Europe they sit in doorways with a dog; in Luxor they shove a baby at you or some big-eyed child raises its hand to its mouth to indicate that it wants food. People who are really in need seldom beg. They go to the mosque or the church to ask for help which they receive as alms. If you see Egyptians giving to a beggar then it is usually a genuine case but if the Egyptians are ignoring them or if they are hanging around tourist spots then you should ignore them too. A team of female beggars work the ferry and the area around Station Street. They always have babies with them. The women get older but the babies never do. In this case begging is a business. Please do not encourage it. Also giving money to children, who are well dressed and well fed and obviously do not need help, only encourages others to turn to begging rather than to work.

Belly Dancing – all Egyptian girls can dance and dance well, as they have been doing it since they were toddlers, but they seldom do it in public; their dancing is reserved for husbands and family. The belly-dancers seen in the hotels are usually foreign women as it is considered a disreputable occupation. Many men are adept at belly-dancing but it is a woman's role. Traditionally men dance with sticks.

Belly Dancing Costumes – can be bought in the tourist souk in Luxor for a fraction of the prices charged in the UK. The finish is not always as good as you would like it to be but the faults are usually easily remedied. The bras and heavy beaded belts do not have fastenings on them as they have 'fit all' sizing that is adjusted through the position of the fastenings. There are no specialist dancing costume emporiums in Luxor like the huge one in the Khan el Khalilli in Cairo and it can be hard to try things on before you buy them but if you return something that proves to be too big or too small and really cannot be adjusted then the shop keeper will usually exchange it.

Benzene – is what the Brits call petrol and Americans call gas. Most of the cars run on benzene while the mini-buses run on diesel. It is available in 90, 92 and 95 grades which are unleaded. There have been massive shortages in recent years and queues can block roads and cause mayhem. Car owners have been known to queue all night, sleeping in their cars, hoping that a delivery will come first thing in the morning. At present, benzene is heavily subsidised and prices are set by the government at 175 piastras (90), 185 piastras (92) and 285 piastras (95). However, the government proposes to introduce a rationing system during 2013 that is based on coupons which allow the purchase of 1800 litres of subsidised fuel. This may replace the chaos of queuing but may create a thriving black-market in coupons. The unsubsidised cost of fuel will multiply threefold or more.

Bicycles – cycling around the west bank is a pleasure as you can get away from the main roads and see the villages. You will not be in any danger although the village children may run after you in excitement at seeing a stranger. Cycling on the east bank is totally different and, unless you have nerves of steel to tackle the traffic, is not recommended. Bicycles can be hired for about 10 LE per day. Remember to lock the bike. If someone steals it you are responsible for its replacement.

Bilharzia – is endemic in the Nile Valley. Water-snail larvae penetrate the skin through small lesions and then move through the body. They are undetectable until the damage is done to your internal organs. There is no preventative method of protection. The larvae are most prevalent in the very quiet stretches of water so the faster stretches will be safe from them but the river has vicious currents and people drown regularly so stay safe and stay out of the Nile. There are swimming pools in the hotels that should fulfil your needs.

Bills – it can be difficult to obtain bills as proof of purchase or to check that what you are being asked to pay for actually matches what you have bought. The best way to do this is through a polite 'fatoura law samaht' ('bill if you please') or a more direct 'aiz fatoura' ('I want a bill').

Bint – is Arabic for 'girl' and is a word brought back to the UK and introduced as slang for girl by soldiers serving in Egypt during the world wars.

Bird Watching – bring your binoculars. Winter in Luxor is a bird watcher's paradise as the migrating birds travel south to the warmer climes of Africa and then travel north again in the spring to the nesting grounds in Europe. Bird books are available in the Gaddis bookshop.

Boat Sales – there are many scams over boat sales so take care if you are considering buying one. Most boats are sold by word of mouth but there is a broker in Luxor that deals with vessels of all sizes. It is called Luxor Marine Services and shares an office with Luxor4u Network Estate Agency near Luxor Temple.

Boats – there are several types of boat on the river: the ferry and the motor boats carry passengers across the river; the ones with sails are either feluccas or dahabyias and cater for tourists wanting leisurely travel; small fishing boats appear at dawn and dusk; and cruise boats travel between Luxor and Aswan. The queens of the River Nile are the antique steam boats.

Bokra – is Arabic for 'tomorrow' and is a word that you will hear often. A shopkeeper will offer to get you anything for tomorrow. Please do not take this too seriously as time means little in Egypt and tomorrow could be in another lifetime.

Book of Gates – is a funerary text and helps the deceased in the passage through the Underworld and is shown on many tombs walls. The journey has a number of gates, each overseen by a goddess and the text gives the spells for passing through each gate. It also outlines the four races of humanity; listed as Egyptians, Libyans, Nubians and Asiatics.

Book of the Dead – the Book of the Dead is not a single book but is a set of funerary texts that were written on coffins, funeral shrouds and the walls of tombs. The texts give the spells necessary for eternal life. These spells were added to over the centuries and by the 18th dynasty the famous spell 125 was added which refers to the weighing of the heart ceremony. Its instructions cover the preservation of the body as well as how to enter the Afterlife and some instructions were inscribed on scarabs to be added to the wrappings of the mummified corpse.

Book Shops – there are some excellent book shops in Luxor selling books on a wide range of subjects but specialising mainly in Egyptology. The Aboudi and Gaddis bookshops are the most well-known and are worth a visit. The Gaddis bookshop is situated close to the Winter Palace. Aboudi has 3 shops in Luxor, one by McDonalds, one in Passport Office Street, opposite the Sonesta, and a small one, specialising in paintings, in the street beside Genesis Bar in Karnak. Second-hand novels tend to be expensive and are offered at their original cover price or even higher so stock up your Kindle or notebook with holiday reading before you leave home.

Borrowing – unless you are prepared to give an item away and to lose it permanently then do not lend it to anyone as once it is out of your sight that is the last you will see of it. The only chance of getting something returned is for you to actually go and knock on the borrower's door and ask for it. The philosophy used is that if you could afford to lend it then you did not need it. This applies to money as a well as goods and to expats as well as Egyptians.

Bougainvillea – is a vividly coloured perennial that can be found all over Luxor. Care needs to be taken when dealing with it as it has nasty spikes on its stems and it is often grown along walls in an effort to discourage intruders.

Boxing – there is an active and competitive boxing club for young people with a professional coach (Ken Robinson) at the sports ground in Tiba which is close to Luxor. It has good support from both male and female members and teaches both traditional boxing and kick boxing. They meet Monday, Wednesday, and Saturday 5 pm at Naadi Sharb

Brass – there are some very good quality brass jugs, trays and ornaments to be found in the souk but haggle fiercely and feel the weight of them before you buy as many are inferior and only brass coloured. Beware of artificially aged items that are sold as antiques at inflated prices.

Bread – the usual way of buying bread ('aish') in Luxor is to get a 1 LE bag of between 4 and 6 long rolls (dependent on the cost and availability of flour). They are similar in taste to European bread and do not have the sweetness that spoils bread in Cairo. The local staple is a pitta type flatbread which is very heavily subsidised at the government approved bakeries. Baladi bread is usually cooked on a weekly basis in large batches in domed mud-ovens. This bread comes in flattish round loaves. The consistency is heavy but it tastes delicious when freshly baked. The larger supermarkets also sell a good range of European style rolls and bread, which is usually sliced and suitable for toasting.

Bread Ovens – there are two types of bread ovens. The most common type is the ancient domed mud-built ovens that are fuelled by burning waste material. 24 loaves can be baked at one time in these ovens on a shelf above the flames. The other type is a gas-fired metal cabinet with shelves.

Breakfast – outside of the luxury hotels, breakfasts normally consist of bread rolls or pitta bread, a hard-boiled egg, a wedge of processed cheese and a small carton of jam (usually fig jam). Egyptians usually eat beans ('foul') and bread at breakfast time.

Breasts – breasts were frequently bared in ancient times but Egypt is an Islamic country and breasts are now completely covered. An exception to the rule is with breast-feeding which can be done openly and without embarrassment. It can be disconcerting to be sitting on the ferry and observe a young mother, who is dressed in a black abyia and hijab, uncover a breast and proceed to feed her child. This is considered fully acceptable and males on the ferry will avert their eyes. Some tourists have a tendency to wear low cut tops revealing cleavage but this is frowned upon.

Bridge over the Nile – the nearest bridge lies 10 km to the south of Luxor and provides the only crossing for vehicles for many miles. There is a police checkpoint at each end.

Brook Clinic - the Brook Clinic has been working in Luxor for decades and concentrates its efforts on working horses and donkeys. It was based at the rear of Luxor Temple but had to move in 2010 following the renovation of the temple area. It is now situated in the old ACE buildings on the edge of town.

Budget Hotels – are easy to find in Luxor as there are always touts handing out business cards at the railway and bus stations.

Buffalos – ('jamoosa') look like big cows with very bony backsides. They provide milk for making yoghurt ('zebadi') and butter ('zebda') for village families and provide an income through the onward sale of calves. When butchered the meat is not hung but is sold immediately and has a tendency to be tough. You can see the legs swinging from hooks outside the butchers' shops. The offal and tails are sold in the souk.

Building – Luxor (2013) looks like one big building site with gaunt unfinished layers of concrete and steel marring the views. Most of the building is illegal and opportunistic due to a lack of policing during the post Mubarak period. Whichever street you go down there will be a pile of sand, bricks or gravel partially blocking your way. In some cases it stays like that for years as building takes place only when money is available and stops as soon as money is exhausted. Luxor has literally thousands of unfinished flats but people still keep building more; some will be built in readiness for sons' families but most are speculative. Local people tolerate the mess but it is an eyesore and far from a pleasing sight to greet tourists. Recently, the illegal coffee shops built close to Luxor Temple were flattened and hopefully the Council will soon get to grips with the problem and remove all the rest of the illegally built structures. Building costs are far lower than in Europe because labour costs are low but as a European you will automatically be charged way above the going price so if you are contemplating building then keep out of the way and let an Egyptian bargain for you. Please take note that building on someone else's land is not saving money; it is giving the landowner a gift of the completed property. Registering a building in someone else's name for any reason whatsoever is also making them richer at your expense.

Bulls – were revered in ancient Egypt and many were sacrificed to the gods in Thebes during the Opet ceremony. There are good reliefs of the bulls being led to their slaughter in the rear chapels of Medinet Habu and there is a well carved procession of fattened bulls on the rear south-west walls of the 1st court of Luxor Temple. The main bull cults were in the north where the Apis bulls were worshipped but there were others. The Buchis cult, which lasted until about 362 CE and represented Ra and Osiris, was centred on Armant to the south of Luxor. The Ptolemies brought the Greek bull worshiping sects together with the Egyptian sects to create a new Serapis deity which was acceptable to both cultures. The Serapeum where the bulls were interred is in Saqqara and is now open to the public after undergoing extensive renovation. There is a small chapel built by Hadrian and dedicated to Serapis in the forecourt of Luxor Temple.

Burglars – as you go around town you cannot help but notice that all ground floor flats have bars at their windows and wrought iron gates over their doors. Shops have pull-down steel shutters. This is purely a precautionary measure as burglaries are no more common in Luxor than elsewhere but it pays to be prudent. Hotel rooms are also subject to burglaries but this is largely opportunistic rather than planned. You too should take precautions by removing temptation. Always lock your door and lock any money or valuables in a safe if there is one or in a hefty suitcase if no safe is available. Dogs are used as a deterrent in the villages but this is not always practical in town.

Bus Stations – the local bus stations for service cars are referred to as 'mogaf' and there are two in Luxor located at opposite edges of the town. Some tourist buses to Hurghada and Cairo can be boarded on a patch of land to the right of the train station (as you face it) but if you are travelling by bus please check carefully on its departure point as there is another bus station close to the airport. If you are on a bus that is not terminating in Luxor then you will most probably be dropped somewhere on the airport road, sometimes in the early hours of the morning, so arrange a pick up if you can.

Buses – can be a good way to travel about Egypt but they do tend to take an indirect route so journeys can be long. However they are cheap and the buses are reasonably comfortable. There are regular services to Cairo, Aswan and Hurghada. Carefully check where the bus leaves from. Tickets to Hurghada cost from 35 LE and to Cairo cost from 80 LE. A new bus service to Cairo via the desert road leaves each evening from near the ferry point on the west bank.

Business Wives – is the term applied to older women who have formed relationships with men much younger than they are. It is not within the Egyptian culture for men to marry women who are older than themselves and so these arrangements are entered into for the business purposes of obtaining visas and money to support their Egyptian families. While this is far from commendable, it is understandable and initially is largely poverty driven but once successful, it can become an unsavoury habit. One Luxor businessman admits financing his businesses by marrying 23 different European women over the space of several years. Another, still in his mid-20, admits to building a small property empire through 8 different women. Sadly few women realise that they are business wives until all their money has gone and they have been side-lined by an Egyptian wife and even then they can remain in total denial of the situation. This is all well documented. Luxor's gigolos are very adept at playing the long game and it can be years before their plans become evident. Usually is it then too late to recover the financial loss. However, if this is treated as a fair exchange for services rendered (new life and sexual attention etc. in exchange for financial benefits) then the loss does not seem so great. (See Gigolos.)

Businesses – tourists are often tempted to invest in business ventures in Luxor as they seem enticingly cheap to set up but the fact is that most of them fail partly because they were disguised scams with escalating costs and constant demands for money but also because if you start a business that appears successful there will be a dozen clones opening in the immediate vicinity almost as soon as you open your doors. Licenses have to be obtained and these can be costly and take months and even years to finalise before a legitimate business can begin to trade.

Butane Gas – cookers in Luxor are fuelled with butane gas from cylinders. Empty cylinders are exchanged for full ones at a cost of between 8 LE and 40 LE depending on whether there is a glut or a shortage in supply. Donkey carts travel around the streets daily banging on the cylinders with spanners to attract attention.

It is not unusual for fights to break out when there has been a shortage and people have actually been killed trying to get one to take home.

Colossi of Memnon

C

Cairo – Currency Notes

Cairo – is the capital of Egypt and lies to the north in the Nile Delta. It can easily be visited from Luxor with arrangements through any Luxor travel company. It is on the river, not on the coast so is not a port. It is one of the most densely populated cities in the world, has a massive traffic problem and is where the pyramids are sited. Crossing the road is a nightmare. You can travel to Cairo by road, rail or air from Luxor although, if travelling by rail, tourists are only allowed to travel on the night trains as they carry guards. The flight takes less than an hour and the train should take 10 hours but has been known to take up to 14 hours. The Egyptian Museum in Tahrir Square holds an incredible number of items that, because of lack of space, are not well displayed but the Tutankhamun artefacts are simply breath-taking. Try and see the collection of Royal Mummies which are in another room and require an extra ticket. (See Royal Mummies). The pyramids and the Sphinx are magnificent and need to be seen for their size to be appreciated. Also a must-see is the vibrant Khan el Khalilli bazaar close to the El Hussein Mosque and if you have time, the Citadel and the City of the Dead.

Calendar – Egypt works on the Gregorian calendar along with most of the world for business and everyday life but its religious calendar differs and dates not from the life of Christ but from the life of the prophet Mohammed.

Callabouche – is a local prison. In Luxor this is situated in Medina Street just past the Fire Station. Prisons are not like European ones so stay out of trouble as it is not somewhere that you would wish to spend any time.

Calleche – is a horse drawn carriage (also known as hantour) and Luxor has too many of them with horses showing varying degrees of neglect. There are ranks of them close to the Winter Palace Hotel and the Iberotel, and many more roving ones on the prowl for business. If you choose to use one please ensure that the horse is healthy and do not overload the carriage with so many people that the horse has to struggle to pull you all along. The costs vary but a short journey will cost a tourist about 10 LE. However, the driver may want to take you to a market that he swears is only open for that day (lie) or a papyrus museum which is actually a shop from which he hopes to get commission. Having agreed a cost he may later say that it was per person and not for your party. Another ploy is to say that he was quoting a price in English pounds and not Egyptian pounds so be very clear about the cost and the itinerary before you get in the carriage. Do not accept an offer to take you to the West Bank sites – not only is it extremely cruel to the horse, it is also illegal.

Calls to Prayer – ('adhan') in Islam are dictated by daylight hours and not by the clock. There are five calls to prayer during the day, the first being at daybreak and the last ('isha') being about two hours after sunset. Ritual washing ('wudu') must be completed before prayers can be made.

Camels – are expensive creatures to buy and in Luxor are no longer used to carry anything other than tourists, although they are used as beasts of burden in the countryside to the south. Rides can be arranged close to the ferry on the west bank. They are not difficult to mount but when you are getting off hold on tight as the camel falls to its knees and almost tosses the rider over its head. There is an old wives' tale that camel's milk has to be fed to twins to stop them turning into cats at night. There has been no explanation of why this is supposed to work.

Camping Sites – for the budget-conscious independent traveller, the Rezeiki camp and hostel can be found on the east bank along the road to Karnak. On the West Bank, El Salaam camp is by the riverbank, about 2 km from the ferry.

Canals – the land of both sides of the river is criss-crossed with canals of varying sizes bringing water from the river to the fields. Most are filled with dirty water and have banks that are covered with rotting litter. It would not be healthy to fall in, but children do swim in them in summer. Despite their mainly deplorable state they are vital for the irrigation of the fields.

Canna Lilies – are big, bold, beautifully coloured and grow like weeds in Luxor reaching heights of 2 metres on good soil.

Canopic Jar – is the name given to the jars that were used by the ancient Egyptians to store the viscera of the dead so that they could be used in the afterlife. The jars are in sets of four. The stoppers of the early jars were usually in human form but by the new kingdom era they showed the four sons of Horus. The jars contained the liver, lungs, stomach and intestines. The heart and brain were not included as the brain was removed from the skull through the nose with a hook and then discarded and the heart was left inside the body ready for the weighing ceremony. This was because they believed that the heart was the seat of the soul, whereas the brain function was unknown. – (See Sons of Horus.)

Capital – the capital of Egypt is now Cairo but that has not always been the case. Over the millennia, the capital has moved between Memphis, Thebes (Luxor), Tanis, Tel el Armana, Pi Ramses, and Alexandria.

Capital Punishment – Egypt retains capital punishment for major crimes. Death is by hanging.

Car Hire – self-drive cars can be hired in Luxor and there are several car hire firms on the east bank but unless you are really familiar with other drivers' lack of respect for the rules of the road then it is best to hire a driver along with the car. Insurance is another problem. Although it is a requirement for renewing licenses, few drivers carry insurance of any kind and, regardless of fault, you would be held responsible for any damage that the hired car might acquire while in your care.

Carnarvon, 5th Earl of – the 5th Earl Carnarvon (1866-1923) had a great interest in Egyptology and financed Howard Carter's excavations in the Valley of the Kings leading to the discovery of the tomb of Tutankhamun in 1922. He died in Cairo of septicaemia from an infected mosquito bite soon after. His Luxor house is at the top of the hill close to the entrance to the Valley of the Kings.

Carnarvon, 8th Earl of - the present 8th Earl of Carnarvon maintains the family's links with Luxor and visits regularly. With Lady Carnarvon, he is joint-patron of the Little Stars Luxor Children's Trust. There is an Egyptian Exhibition at Highclere Castle his ancestral home in Berkshire UK and a new exhibit showing the tomb of Tutankhamun as it was originally found has recently been added to the displays. Lady Carnarvon has written several books about Carter and the 5th Earl finding Tutankhamun's tomb. Highclere Castle is used as the estate of the Grantham family in the TV series Downton Abbey

Carter – Howard Carter (1874-1939), an Englishman, was an accomplished painter and draughtsman. He was appointed as the first chief inspector of the Egyptian Antiquities Service in 1899 and began working with Lord Carnarvon excavating in the Valley of the Kings in 1914 but the work was interrupted by the outbreak of the WWI. The discovery of the intact tomb of Tutankhamun in 1922 was of international importance and journalists flooded into Luxor to write about it. The relics from the tomb are the greatest attraction at the Egyptian Museum in Cairo.

Carter's House – is the house that Howard Carter lived in while excavating in the Valley of the Kings. It lies at the bottom of the hill close to the road to the Valley of the Kings and not at the top of the hill as many people assume. The house is of mud brick and was renovated in 2010. Inside, there is an excellent hologram presentation of Carter discussing his work. Unfortunately the projector is not always working and, as the guard does not speak English, it is hard to enquire about its state of repair so be prepared for the disappointment of not seeing it. There was a coffee shop on site but it closed due to lack of custom after the 2011 revolution. The house is open to the public but tickets have to be bought at the ticket office and cannot be bought on site. There is a proposal for accurate facsimiles of the tombs of Seti I, Tutankhamun and Queen Nefertari to be made and sited near the Carter House.

Cartouche – A cartouche has an oval shape and is usually shown vertically with a horizontal line at the end. Originally, they were only used to portray the names of Pharaohs and they appeared in their temples, statues, tombs and coffins. It was believed that if your name was written down somewhere then your existence now, and in the Afterlife, was assured. In contrast, destroying someone's name deprived them of an Afterlife. Pharaoh had five titles, two of which were always and uniquely written in a cartouche. One, the 'nomen' or birth name, is surmounted by a sun disk which is the symbol of the god Ra and by a duck which is the symbol for son. So the Pharaoh was the 'Son of Ra'. The second name to appear in a cartouche is the 'prenomen' or coronation name. This is surmounted by a sedge plant which is the hieroglyph for Upper Egypt and a bee which is the hieroglyph for King of Lower Egypt and so named him as 'King of Upper and Lower Egypt'. This pair of cartouches is found all over the walls of temples and tombs, indicating who the owner is, but that does not mean that they were the original owners. Pharaohs were exceedingly avaricious and had a tendency to usurp their predecessors work by carving their own cartouches over earlier ones. Cartouches are now commonly available as tourist souvenirs either as jewellery or papyrus, where you can have your name inscribed in hieroglyphs.

Cash Machines – there are many cash machines in Luxor mainly outside the banks at the southern end of the Corniche and in Khaled Ibn el Walid Street. You will also find them inside all of the major hotels. Keep a strict record of all your transactions as sometimes, if the machine has run out of notes, the transaction will not be completed but the money may have been withdrawn from your account anyway. This is a common and costly problem with the machines of the Bank Misr. If you can, choose a machine in, or outside, an operating bank then it will be easier to recover your card if the machine swallows it.

Cat – ('gotta' or 'bessa'). In ancient Egypt cats were revered but now Luxor's streets are overrun with underfed feral moggies. Egyptians tolerate cats without making pets of them. The cats tend to have long legs and biggish ears. They come and go as they please and live on scraps and things they can steal from kitchen bins. Unless they hang about restaurants and coffee shops, they fear humans and are not usually approachable. There are examples of mummified cats in the Mummification Museum on the Corniche.

Cat Food - The newer supermarkets have become accustomed to foreigners' love of animals and now stock cat food but these are bought mainly by expats not by locals and are very expensive. Many consider it immoral to feed a cat on meat or fish when so many people cannot afford to buy it for their families.

Catholicism – Catholics are a minority within a minority in Egypt but are well catered for in Luxor as there are several Catholic Churches in the town. The main Catholic Church is in Temple Karnak Street.

Chai – is 'tea' and Egyptians like their tea strong, very sweet and without milk. The tea itself is black and in fine granules rather than leaves and can now be obtained in tea bags.

Charities – there are many charities operating in Luxor. The majority are Islamic based such as the ones run by the Muslim Brotherhood and the Society for Development which have done excellent work in the relief of poverty over the last few years. There are also very successful Coptic groups like the Coptic Home for Orphaned Girls and the Good Samaritan Home for the Disabled. There are European based children's charities such as Little Stars and Sunshine which have dual registration and Little Pyramid which is a German organisation. The Brook Clinic and ACE do excellent work with working animals. All are worthy of support.

Checkpoints – there are checkpoints all around Luxor's boundaries on both sides of the river. The guards have varying degrees of attentiveness and some on the west bank can be aggressive, especially after dark. However, ultimately this is all done for your own safety so it is prudent to be patient. If you are visiting sites outside the city area it is best to have a photocopy of your passport details and present visa with you so that it can be inspected if required. It is probably safer to leave the original in your hotel.

Chicago House – is the Luxor centre of the Oriental Institute of Chicago University. It occupies a lovely old house on the Corniche and has an excellent reference library which, by prior appointment, is open to the public during their season in Luxor.

Chick Peas – are actually beans rather than peas (Garbanzo Beans) and play a large part in the Egyptian diet. They are the main ingredient of falafel and kushari. They are also soaked and eaten as a snack (those bright yellow beans they sell close to the ferry). You need to squeeze the soft bean out of its skin to eat it.

Chickens – not long ago all the chickens ('firakh') in Luxor disappeared as panic spread about bird flu. Sadly this led to the demise of the pelicans and the flamingos at the Sheraton Hotel. Recently live chickens have been back on the market and are greatly preferred to the frozen ones which are mainly imported from Brazil. You will see delicious spit roasted chickens outside most Egyptian restaurants and these can be bought to take away.

Childbirth – the infant mortality rate in Egypt is now fairly low with 24 deaths per 1,000 births (2012) which is less than half of what it was only a decade ago but is still nearly 5 times as high as in Europe. There is a slightly higher mortality rate in male babies than in female babies. Except in the outer villages, most babies are now born in hospital or doctors' surgeries with the mother being discharged within 24 hours. Traditionally, women return to their father's home to be helped by their mothers for 40 days after giving birth or until all post-natal bleeding has ceased. During this time, women are not allowed to pray or visit the mosque.

Children – Egyptians love children and consequently have large families which are, by European standards, almost totally undisciplined. There are well behaved children but they appear to be in the minority. Often parents will just stand by and smile as their offspring insult you or demand money. It is pointless getting angry as this usually just makes the behaviour worse as the children vie for your attention. Ignore them completely or just say 'Imshee' – 'Go away'. Young children are delightful and girls can remain so but the boys get used to being princes inside their homes and can act like tyrants outside of them. Do not be surprised to see boys of about 10 or 12 years old driving cars, riding motor bikes with their friends on the back, or driving calleches. This is against the law but usually goes unchecked and unpunished.

Chinese Imports – Chinese imports have displaced many of the cheaper souvenirs on offer in the bazaars and local crafts have suffered. Local people shy away from anything made in China as they believe that China sends them their rubbish. Following a 2012 visit to China by President Mohammed Morsi, an increase in Chinese tourists is anticipated.

Chinese Restaurants – there are several Chinese restaurants in Luxor, the Fortune Cookie in Medina Street, close to St. Joseph Street, being the most well-known.

Chit Chats – are geckos and get their name from the "ch" sound that they make when they communicate with each other. They usually lurk behind pictures and eat insects so they are worth keeping. Egyptians are nervous of them and believe they carry disease but while it is not recommended that they tramp about in your food, they are harmless. Their feet are suckered which allows them to climb walls and walk across the ceiling. All rooms in Luxor have them somewhere or other so learn to love them. (See Geckos.)

Christianity – is one of the religions of 'the book' and is accepted in Egypt but it is an offence to lure people away from Islam so be careful if you feel the need to 'spread the word'. There are Protestant, Catholic and Coptic churches in Luxor.

Christmas – is on 7th January in Luxor and not 25th December as in Europe. It is a Coptic holiday and is celebrated with mass at the Santa Maria Cathedral and in the Catholic churches. However, the major hotels and European style restaurants do have tourist related festivities on the 25th December.

Cinemas – a cinema has recently been opened on the top floor of the shopping mall towards the station end of the Station

Street, (opposite the BTEC electrical shop) but at the moment it only shows Egyptian films. There were plans to site a cinema off the Movenpick Road, close to the Culture Palace but this has not yet come about. However, there is a thriving trade in pirated films in Luxor and several restaurants and expat groups have film nights showing newly released films that have been downloaded from the Internet. Recently, film festivals have come to Luxor. The Luxor African Film Festival and the Egyptian/European Film Festival are held in the Culture Palace in Awamia and in other venues throughout the city.

Civil Marriages – details of the papers required and the formalities to be observed for marriages to take place in Egypt between two British subjects and British subjects marrying Egyptian nationals are given on the UK in Egypt website. For other nationalities, look at your Embassy website and follow the instructions given. (See Orfi.)

Cleopatra – has little connection with Luxor but is of interest to most visitors to Egypt and there are images thought to be of her in the Hathor Temple in Dendera and in the Temple of Horus at Edfu. Although commonly known as Cleopatra, she was actually the 7th of that name and, having committed suicide (30 BCE) was the last of the Ptolemaic Pharaohs to govern Egypt. Cleopatra had a son by Julius Caesar and three children by Mark Antony. There are no temples to Cleopatra but the Egyptian archaeologist Zahi Hawass believes that he may have found her tomb at Taposiris Magna near Alexandria (to be verified) and there has been extensive work in Alexandria's harbour in recovering statues which may have come from her palace. She was the only Ptolemaic Pharaoh to bother to learn the Egyptian language.

Cleopatra Ceramics – makes bathroom suites and floor tiles and employs around 20,000 people. Almost every ceramic sink, toilet and floor in Luxor will have the Cleopatra brand mark on it somewhere.

Cleopatra Cigarettes – are cheap and easily obtainable throughout Luxor. Egypt was a major exporter of cigarettes in the 19th century but now only produces cigarettes for domestic consumption. Many Egyptian males are heavy smokers.

Clothing – during the day, as the sun is fierce, Luxor can be very hot at all times of the year. You will be coolest wearing loose clothing made of natural fibres. Skimpy tops should be avoided as they not only offend local customs but may also give the wrong impression as to your morality. They also let you get very badly sunburned. There is an abundance of tops for sale in the souk at very reasonable prices. Haggle.

Clothing Shops – there is a glut of men's clothing shops in Luxor and with the fall in tourist numbers all of them are struggling; not because they catered for tourists but because the local men, who used to buy the fancier clothes, work in the tourist trade and they themselves are now short of money.

Coffee – if you ask for coffee in a local coffee shop you will be served Turkish coffee in a small glass with an accompanying glass of water. If you want western style coffee then you should ask for 'Nescafe'. It is a generic term for all the powdered coffees. Freshly brewed filtered coffees can only be found in the hotels and up-market coffee shops and restaurants.

Coffee Shops – coffee shops are a vital addition to Egyptian culture as Egyptian men seem to spend an extraordinary amount of time in them smoking shishas and playing dominoes. Tables spill out onto the pavements into the small hours of the morning. Women are seldom seen in them. There are several European style coffee shops but most coffee shops sell only Turkish coffee, instant Nescafe sachets or the inferior Egyptian ones.

Colonnade – the magnificent colonnade in Luxor Temple was constructed by Amenhotep III and has seven pairs of 16m high papyrus topped columns. The walls of the colonnade, sadly in quite poor condition, depict the Opet festival and were the work of Tutankhamen when he abandoned the Aten and reinstated the old religion. His image appears at the beginning of the procession (north-west wall section) but the cartouches are those of his successor Horemheb who unashamedly usurped most of Tutankhamun's work there and elsewhere.

Colossi of Memnon – are two giant statues of Amenhotep III which stand in splendid isolation close to the Theban Hills on the road past the crossroads checkpoint. Originally they fronted his magnificent temple. One is carved from a single block of stone and the other is in five layers. There are small effigies of his wife and mother at his feet. The statues were misnamed by the Greeks who thought that they represented Memnon, a hero of the Trojan wars. They were severely damaged in an earthquake in the early Roman era which left one with a low moan usually heard as the air warmed up following the dawn. Memnon was the son of Aurora, goddess of the dawn, who supposedly wept for him after his death at Troy - hence the attribution of the statues. They were restored several times in antiquity and eventually repairs ensured the statues cried no more. Proposals are being considered for them to be restored again.

Colour – the temple and tomb walls were usually brightly coloured and visitors are often amazed by the degree to which these colours have stood the test of time. Those in shaded areas are particularly vivid. The ancient Egyptians used various mineral-based pigments: white from limestone; black from charcoal; yellow and red ochres (oxides of iron); blue (from azurite, an oxide of copper) and green (from malachite, another oxide of copper).

Columns – many people already recognise the lotus and papyrus topped columns but there are many more styles and sometimes there are several different styles within one temple. Papyrus-topped columns are those most frequently found in Luxor. The opened buds top the columns in the Hypostyle Hall at Karnak and the Colonnade at Luxor Temple. Closed-bud tops can also be found in both temples. Lotus-topped columns were more a feature in Ptolemaic temples and can be seen at Dendera, Edfu and Aswan. In addition, there are Hathor topped columns that show the goddess with a female head and cows ears. You can see these in the Opet Temple at Karnak, the Hathor Temple at

Deir el Medina and in the Hathor Chapel in Hatshepsut's Temple at Deir el Bahri. They would all have been brightly coloured and would have looked stunning even in the darkness of a hypostyle hall.

Computers – Luxor is well provided with shops selling computer accessories. There is an outlet selling used Dell computers in Television Street in what was the old Mish Mish Restaurant. There is a computer shop called Luxor Digital just off Medina Street, close to Omar Market which has a repair service as well as stocking PCs, laptops etc. There is an excellent shop in Manshia, opposite Amoun Digital, but watch the steps. On the west bank, Future Net offers internet access, as well as computer and accessory sales.

Condoms – locally bought condoms are not very reliable or effective so bring your own with you if you intend to have sex.

Conference Centre – the Conference Centre is on the Corniche on the corner of the turning that goes up to the airport. There are rumours that it will be demolished in a road widening scheme but has so far escaped unscathed.

Consul – there are no British consuls or consulate services in Luxor. Mr Ehab Gaddis served as the UK Honorary Consul for many years but resigned when there was a change in Egyptian law that made it impossible to carry on in the role. He has not been replaced and is continuing with the role but without the title. A warden system of passing on vital information is being planned.

Contraception – in ancient Egypt, among other things, crocodile dung was mixed with honey and formed into a pessary to use as a contraceptive. Acacia gum was also used which was likely to be more effective as acacia has been found to be spermicidal. Egypt now has an uncontrolled population explosion and a weak family planning programme. Barrier contraceptives are frowned upon but not forbidden and are of low quality. However, oral contraceptives are considered acceptable as they are 'medicines' but they are financially out of reach to many village women. Many Egyptian women are now fitted with an IUD (inter-uterine device) such as a coil but again this method is not widely available to village women because either they are not aware of it or are not able to travel to a clinic to have one fitted.

Convoys – convoys ran for years between Luxor, Hurghada and Aswan but these ceased in 2010 allowing freedom of travel during daylight hours. However, following some kidnapping and robberies on the routes, the convoys were temporarily reinstated but have been discontinued at the time of writing. Although the convoys are for tourist protection they are dangerous as they travel at breakneck speeds through the winding mountain roads and there are frequent accidents. Although it may be an unfair criticism, the police could be the main cause of this as they lead the convoys and they set the pace at which they travel.

Copper – while some of the copper trays and jugs in the souk are of inferior quality there are some wonderful hand-engraved plaques and plates available. They are very heavy though and may need to be forwarded to you rather than taken home in your luggage. Haggle fiercely as the first price put forward is usually ridiculously high.

Copts – the apostle Mark came to Egypt in 56 CE and was martyred there in 68 CE. He established the Coptic Church of Alexandria which was one of the earliest Christian movements. Today, approximately 10% of Egypt's population follows the Coptic faith. Although the Copts and the Muslims live side by side, and there is normally not a lot of sectarian violence between the two groups, there is an underlying mistrust. Copts have their own Pope and Pope Shenouda who was greatly loved died in 2011. He was replaced by Pope Tawadros II in November 2012. The largest Coptic Church in Luxor is the lovely Santa Maria Cathedral in Temple Karnak Street.

Corniche – is technically called the Corniche el Nil but is commonly referred to simply as the Corniche. It is the wide promenade that runs along the eastern side of Nile between Karnak and the roundabout at the Iberotel and is a pleasant area to walk and sit in the cool of the evening. Unfortunately it is also a haunt for touts and gigolos so there can be a lot of hassle. As part of the proposed pedestrianisation of the entire Corniche, (with the exception of taxis, calleches and the emergency services) a new, landscaped section has been built from the Luxor Museum to the Conference Centre.

Creation Myths – as in all cultures and religions there are numerous myths offering explanations for the creation of the universe. One creation myth relating to Thebes proposes that the Ogdoad (group of eight primary gods) oversaw the laying of an egg at Medinet Habu from which sprang the bird of light and the creation god Ra.

Credit Cards – be wary of using credit cards in shops as there has been a reported increase in cloning and subsequent credit card fraud. Also, as Luxor is very much a cash-based economy, very few shops accept them. Most credit cards can be used to withdraw local currency from the cash machines which could prove safer. (See Cash Machines.)

Crime – the crime rate involving tourists used to be very low but rose during the period of lawlessness that followed the revolution. The majority of crimes appear to be of petty theft and sexual assault but more serious cases of kidnapping and robbery have occurred in the Sinai area. Reported cases of rape are rare but unreported rape does occur. The police are now (early 2013) back on the streets following the election of a new President but are still largely ineffective.

Crows – hooded crows are among the most common birds that you will see in Luxor. They are grey with black heads that look like an executioner's hood. Their wings are also black and they strut about as though they were peacocks instead of scavenging carrion crows.

Cruises – run between Luxor and Aswan and there is a lock to be negotiated at Esna. The route from Cairo to Aswan was recently restored but, being extremely expensive, was abandoned through lack of support. It is due to start service again in the

2013-14 season but tourist numbers are still very low. There are over 300 boats on the river ranging from modern cruise boats to restored antique steam boats. Cruises can be booked locally. Ask about the other passengers when booking as many boats tend to be booked by one nationality or another and it can be uncomfortable if you are the only person on board who speaks your language.

Cultural Palace – the Cultural Palace was situated close to the Old Winter Palace Hotel but was demolished in the remodelling of Luxor. The new Cultural Palace is a splendid pink building on the Movenpick Road. It was used recently as a venue for the Luxor African and the International Film Festivals. The new building suffered superficial damage during the first days of the revolution but this was quickly repaired.

Currency – the Egyptian currency is the pound normally referred to as LE. It is a decimal system, split into 100 parts, known as piastras.

Currency Coins – although tourists do not usually see them, the coinage in Luxor ranges from 5 piastras right though to one pound. The coins decrease in size or weight as their value falls and are in varying metals. The one pound coin is a bi-metal combination coloured silver and gold.

Currency Exchange – it is better to change money into the local currency on arrival in Egypt as the exchange rate is very much better. All the major banks have currency exchange counters except the Bank of Abu Dhabi in Khaled Ibn el Walid Street which has a currency exchange machine outside. The exchange rate between the GBP Pound and the Egyptian Pound is dependent on the exchange rate between the GBP and the American Dollar. The exchange rate hovered slightly above the 9.50 LE to GBP rate for most of 2012 but in early 2013 the exchange rate between the Dollar and the Egyptian pound fell to an eight year low and this affected the exchange rates for other currencies leading to a rate of 10.00 – 10.50 LE to the GBP. Forecasts predicted a massive fall in the value of the Egyptian pound but this has not actually happened.

Currency Notes – the lower value notes tend to be very dog-eared and grubby but it pays to have a wad of them available for tips etc. The lowest value note is 10 piastras and then they progress through to 200 LE which is the highest value in common use. The progression is 10 piastras, 25 piastras, and 50 piastras, then 1 LE, 5 LE, 10 LE, 20 LE, 50 LE, 100 LE and finally 200 LE. There are two sizes of 200 LE notes in circulation which can be confusing so take care when using them. High value notes with tears in them are likely to be rejected by smaller shops but repaired tears in smaller value notes are acceptable. Getting change is difficult and can take an extraordinary length of time to obtain, so make sure you have small notes in your wallet as well as large ones. Be particularly on your guard against scammers switching (with conjuror-like skill) the note you gave them and then claiming you gave them a smaller one.

The Temple of Hatshepsut at Deir el Bahri

D

Dahabyia – Duty Free

Dahabyia – is a shallow draft Nile boat with two lateen sails which was used by 19th century visitors like Florence Nightingale and Amelia Edwards, author of "A Thousand Miles Up The Nile". The boats were generally superseded by steam cruisers, and the modern cruise ships, but many have survived as a more relaxed and exclusive holiday cruise. There are several dahabyia holiday companies in Luxor although many of the boats are moored at Esna. The boats are generally wind dependent and need a tug to tow them when the wind strength is low, but the dahabyias owned by the major tour companies do have on-board engines.

Dairy Produce – although fresh milk ('leban') is available in Luxor, most shops only sell UHT milk in cartons. You can get fresh butter ('zebda'), yoghurt ('zebadi') and goats' cheese ('feta') as well as a wide range of hard cheeses ('jibna') in any supermarket. Cartons of UHT milk are now available in full-cream, half-cream and skimmed varieties. Flavoured yoghurts and drinking yoghurts made by international companies are also easily found. (Soya milk is available in some supermarkets for those who are not dairy tolerant.)

Dancing – there are several forms of dancing displays to be seen in Luxor. Performances of Stick-Dancing by men and Belly-Dancing by women are sometimes given in the major hotels and can often be seen at local weddings. In addition, there is Sufi Dancing in the form of the Whirling Dervish (called 'Tanour') that can be seen regularly at the Nile Palace and the Gaddis Hotels. The original Sufi dancers were seeking religious perfection but now it is done for entertainment and it is well worth watching. The dancers wear heavy multi-coloured skirts and whirl continuously while manipulating the skirt in a colourful display. (See Belly Dancing.)

Date Palms – dot the landscape in and around Luxor but there are no large date plantations as there are in the north of the country. Not just the fruit of the palm is used. The spines of the fronds are used for making baskets and light furniture such as cane tables, chairs and beds and the trunks are split to make roof beams for traditional mud brick houses.

Dates – ('balalh') there are several types of dates on offer in the local markets. They vary in sweetness, colour and price. Some can cost 1 or 2 LE per kilo while other imported varieties can cost up to 20 LE per kilo.

Daylight Saving – in order to extend daylight hours during the summer months, an hour was added to local time between the end of April and the end of September each year. It was introduced during WW2 and was abolished in 1945 but was reintroduced in 1957. It remained until 2011 when Ramadan fell in the summer months. The extended hour of fasting caused great hardship so it was abolished again; this time probably permanently.

Days of the week – ('youm') in Egypt the days of the week are numbered instead of named. Sunday is day one ('Youm al Ahad') and a day of rest for Christians. Monday is day two ('Youm al Itnayn'). Tuesday is day three (Youm al Talat) and market day. Wednesday and Thursday are days four and five. In Islam, Friday is a day of prayer and is known as 'day six' but also as 'al juma'. Saturday is day seven.

Dehydration – can easily be avoided by drinking freely. Bottled water can be bought almost anywhere. Your urine should be clear and copious and if it is dark and sludgy then you are causing problems for your kidneys. Rehydration salts can be bought cheaply at any pharmacy but it is better to drink water frequently and use salt on your food to avoid the problem.

Deir – is a tag given to several ancient monuments in the necropolis. It means 'Monastery' and denotes that the place was once a place of Coptic worship. Several of Luxor's temples were used in this way.

Deir el Bahri – the 'Northern Monastery', is the name given to the Mortuary Temple of Hatshepsut. The temple rises out of the landscape in a series of terraces which were once covered with plants. It is one of the earliest temples in the west bank necropolis and has undergone extensive restoration work. There is a chapel to Hathor on the second level and several statues of Hatshepsut in the form of Osiris. As the name suggests, the temple was once used as a Coptic place of worship. The reliefs in this temple are now very difficult to see except in the raking early morning or late afternoon light. At midday they are almost invisible so pick your visiting time carefully. (See Hatshepsut.)

Deir el Medina – means 'Monastery of the Town' and is the name given to the Village of the Tomb Builders (Workers) which nestles in a small valley close to the Valley of the Queens. Its name derives from when it had a Coptic Monastery on the hill above the village. There is a small but delightful Ptolemaic temple there which is devoted to Hathor. The village has been extensively restored to show its layout but there are no remains of the monastery. However, there is a Coptic cross carved into the Temple's outer wall and Greek graffiti close to its entrance. The temple and three tombs are open to the public. (See Workers' Village.)

Dendera – there is a very well preserved Ptolemaic temple to Hathor at Dendera. Most visitors reach it by road but there is also a day-cruise from Luxor which is very interesting and relaxing. The cruise takes 4 hours which is a good opportunity to see life on the riverbank and allows you to spend one and half hours at the temple before returning. There are reliefs showing Cleopatra in the temple and there was a famous Zodiac (a circular bas relief depicting the heavens) on the ceiling of one of the Osiris chapels. This was removed to France in 1821, with the blessing of the Egyptian ruler Mohamed Ali Pasha, and is now in the Louvre. A replica has been put in its place but Egypt is asking for the return of the original.

Dentists – there is a reliable expat favoured dentist called Farid Shawky in Cleopatra Street which is off the Tourist Souk and one called Fawky Henary on the corner opposite Abu el Haggag Square.

Deportations – when you get into a serious dispute with an Egyptian you may be threatened with being 'thrown out of the country'. This is an empty threat as deportations are rare and hard to arrange. Undesirable foreign residents are also seldom deported and are just refused re-entry once they have left the country for any reason.

Deserts – Egypt is 95% barren desert but the ones that are of interest to tourists are the Red and White deserts which are in the north but can be reached from Luxor via the new desert road. Most of the tour companies will arrange individual or small group safari-type tours where you can visit the oases and sleep under the stars.

Desserts – Egyptian desserts tend to be sugar saturated and very sweet but favourite local desserts also favoured by tourists are Om Ali and Kanafa.

Diabetes – is a major problem in Egypt with up to 17% of the population being affected by either type 1 or type 2 diabetes, (WHO report Dec 2012). The problem is greater in men than in women and is exacerbated by Egypt's rampant 'sugar addiction'. Insulin is expensive and few can afford it, consequently few sufferers are receiving medication. Due to shared needles, there is a high Hep C rate in those that do inject insulin.

Dialects – there any many dialects in Egypt and classic Arabic is not really spoken anywhere outside of the elite. The Luxor dialect is very guttural and in some cases almost incomprehensible even to Cairenes. CD-based Language courses in Arabic tend to work on a Jordanian version of Arabic that is not really relevant to that spoken in Luxor. There is even a difference between west bank and east bank pronunciation of some words.

Diarrhoea – the most common ailment to afflict visitors is diarrhoea which comes from contaminated food, poor hygiene and a change of water. Much of the advice given on Traveller's Information sites is alarmist. You are not going to get dysentery from eating salad in a restaurant in Luxor; all you will do is deny yourself the pleasure of eating fresh vegetables and it is perfectly safe to use tap water to clean your teeth. You can get a stomach upset from a change of water and that includes drinking mineral water if your body is not used to it. The main source of infection is probably rice. Yes, it is tasty but it is also a breeding ground for bacteria. As a remedy drink lots of water and if possible let the infection pass through you rather than trapping it in with medication that paralyses the bowel. Antinal is the local effective antibiotic and is available at all the pharmacies. Diarrhoea is a major health problem in Egyptian babies and children.

Diesel – known locally as Gas or 'Solar'.

Disabled Visitors – sadly, Luxor is not disability-friendly. The pavements are high and most of the smaller hotels only have stairs for access. Few concessions have been made in the historic sites to accommodate tourists with disabilities. Moves are being made to try and improve matters but progress is slow. There are several disabled parking places around the town but they usually have non-disability vehicles double parked in them.

Disco – there is not much 'night life' in Luxor as Europeans would understand the term. There is a disco every Thursday night at the Gaddis Hotel in Khaled Ibn el Walid Street and an intermittent one in the El Luxor (Etap) Hotel on the Corniche but few other provisions exist.

Diving – in the Red Sea is very popular as there are many diving schools in Hurghada which is within easy reach of Luxor. The cost of courses and PADI certification is far lower than in Europe.

Divorce – is always sad as it means that a relationship has broken down. Divorce is not possible in Coptic marriages but is remarkably easy in Muslim marriages. Muslim men are allowed four wives at any one time, although few ever have more than one, and are able to divorce their wives simply by stating three times in public, the intention to divorce and then registering it with the authorities following a mandatory three month waiting period to ascertain that the woman being divorced is not pregnant. Divorced women are allowed to keep their wedding gold and the items of furniture etc. that they brought to the marriage. Women can divorce their husbands but this is a very lengthy process and the woman may lose her children and leave the marriage with nothing.

Djinns – are supernatural spirits and are mentioned in the Koran (the unseen made of smokeless fire). Belief in djinns is still prevalent. They have free will and can be good, malevolent or neutral but most people think of them as being malevolent and will ask the help of a sheikh to dislodge them if they think one has moved into their house. Salt is often sprinkled around rooms and beds as protection against them.

Doctors – the general GP type of doctor found in Europe is scarce in Luxor. Doctor training is relatively short so they specialise in chosen areas early on and you will need to seek one that matches your ailment. If you are really feeling ill then it might be best to go to the International Hospital and ask for advice from the doctors on duty. There is a fee but it is not onerous. There is also a new Medical Centre in St. Joseph's Street which has an out-patient consultancy service.

Dogs – ('kalb') - there are a lot of dogs protecting property in the villages on both sides of the river. They are bad tempered and are not to be petted. The large packs that used to roam the streets have been dealt with mainly by poisoning, which some Europeans find upsetting. There is rabies in Egypt and if you are bitten by a dog seek medical attention. Egyptians do not keep dogs as pets as many consider them to be dirty and will not touch them.

Dominoes – the game of dominoes is a national pass-time and the loud clack of a slapped down domino can be heard constantly when you are close to any coffee shop. The game is taken very seriously.

Donkeys – are kept only as working animals. They carry everything from sugar cane and building materials through to people and are harnessed to carts pulling incredibly heavy loads. Sadly they are not always well cared for and ACE and Brook are kept busy trying to bring neglected and abused animals back to health. Donkey rides are available on the west bank.

Driving – in Luxor is not for the timid motorist. You need to be pushy and have nerves of steel to tackle Luxor's traffic problems. Local drivers have low regard for rules and although technically they drive on the right, they actually drive wherever they please. In addition, you have to deal with suicidal pedestrians who put their faith in Allah rather than common sense, calleches, motor bikes and wayward donkey carts plus huge potholes and collapsed drains. Overtaking is aggressive. Egypt has one of the highest traffic accident death rates in the world and Luxor is not an exception.

Drugs – are available in Egypt and bango is often openly smoked but the penalty for trafficking is a death sentence. Say 'NO" to drugs!

Dust Storms – are frequent in Luxor especially during the spring when the 'Khamseen' winds blow from the Sahara. The wind can reach speeds of 140 km per hour and the air can become so thick with dust that it burns the eyes and makes it difficult to see. They are usually short-lived but have occasionally been known to last for several days and will find every crack in the brickwork to cover you and your accommodation with a layer of fine sand.

Duty Free – you can buy Duty Free items up to 48 hours after you land in Luxor. There is a duty-free shop at the airport, as well as two in Luxor – (one in Karnak and one in Awamia not far from the KFC.) The old duty free shop in the town centre has recently closed. Allowances appear to depend on who is serving you and how much can be made on the appalling rates of exchange that the shops offer if paying in anything other than US dollars.

The Temple of Khnum at Esna

E
Eagles - Expats

Eagles – eagles have been seen flying along the riverbank but they are now a rarity. There is a stylised eagle in a white band in the middle of the Egyptian flag and, along with the vulture, eagles feature prominently in ancient Egyptian religions and art. The eagle represents power and freedom.

East Bank – the eastern side of the River Nile is where the Government Offices and most of the shops are situated. The pace of life is faster and the traffic thicker than on the west bank and which side you choose to stay is a matter of taste. With the exception of the El Moudira Hotel all the 5* hotels are on the east bank and so are most of the best restaurants. The town area stretches from Karnak in the north to Awamia in the south.

Easter – Easter is celebrated later in Luxor than in Europe.

easyJet – is a scheduled airline and has flights into Luxor from London Gatwick on both Mondays and Wednesdays during the high season. They are a low budget airline with limited baggage allowance but they offer a good service. Tickets can be booked over the Internet.

Egrets – are common in Egypt and can be seen pecking in the fields. Many visitors think that they are sacred ibis but sadly they are not. There are no sacred ibis left in Egypt. At sunset the trees along the riverbank can turn white with the vast number of cattle-egrets that roost in them. It is a magnificent sight.

Egypt Air – the Egypt Air offices are on the Corniche close to the Winter Palace Hotel. As well as an International service they have several daily domestic flights to Cairo, Aswan and Sharm el Sheikh. Their flights to and from the UK are on Mondays only and fly from Heathrow. They are in the Star Alliance so be careful when you book a flight that you opt for the correct airline as Egypt Air have a much larger baggage allowance (2 x 23 kg bags) than other Alliance members which only allow 1 x 20 kg bag.

Egyptian Food – is spiced and usually delicious but there may be too much salt in it for some European tastes. Among the favourite dishes are Kushari, Falafel, Shawarma, Targen, Kromb, Stuffed Pigeon and various dishes containing local aubergines.

Egyptologists – many foreign and Egyptian Egyptologists work on numerous sites in the Luxor area throughout the winter months. However, you cannot visit any of their sites without prior permission from the MSA (Ministry of State for Antiquities). Often, the Egyptologists give lectures or seminars on their work, and also have online blogs detailing their day-to-day activities. Very few actually live in the Luxor area, but Kent Weeks who is one of the most prominent Luxor Egyptologists, spends much of the year there.

Eid – there are two Eid festivals in the Islamic calendar. Both are considered times of celebration and there are often fairs and parties. Eid el Fitre follows Ramadan and Eid el Adha, which takes place a few months later, celebrates Abraham's sacrifice and involves the mass slaughter of sheep. Luxor closes down for 3 days at each of the festivals. In the villages it is a time for socialising and families either visit or welcome their neighbours offering cakes and sweet treats. Traditionally, children receive new clothes at Eid and families sometimes take bags of oranges to the cemeteries to share with others in memory of their dead relatives. There is an Eid greeting in the form of 'kol senna wa inta tayeb' meaning 'may you be well all year'; it is bit like 'happy new year'.

El Hussein Street – El Hussein Street runs off Karnak Temple Street and is on the service car route. There are several hotels there including the Emilio and the Venus hotels. The street is crossed by the Tourist Souk on one side and the Egyptian Market on the other.

El Luxor Hotel – used to be called the Etap and it still known locally by that name. It is a 5* hotel and is situated on the

Corniche. Some rooms have Nile views. In addition to the usual restaurants there is an intermittent disco with a minimum charge which has displays of belly-dancing.

El Mesala Hotel – is a fairly new hotel with a swimming pool, situated close to the West Bank ferry point. It is the only hotel on the West Bank built facing the Nile, and has great views of Luxor Temple from some of its rooms and from its restaurant.

El Tod – there is a mainly Ptolemaic temple to Montu at El Tod which is about 20 km south west of Luxor on the east bank. Tickets for this temple are sold at the Luxor Temple Ticket Office so please get one before you travel down there. There were temples dating back to the 5th dynasty but little or nothing of those now remain.

Electricity – runs on a round 2 pin system with 220-240 volts so all European gadgets and chargers will run with an adaptor (which cost between 2 LE and 5 LE in Luxor). However, the system is very unreliable and there are frequent cuts with surges when power is restored. If you have something plugged in when the power is cut then unplug it as it could burn out when the power flows again. Egyptian plugs do not have fuses and the system is unearthed.

Embara – is Arabic for yesterday. 'Embara lail' is 'last night'.

Embassy – there are few if any Embassy officials of any nationality in Luxor now (although the British Embassy sometimes has a clinic with visiting officials answering questions). So if you have any problems over passports or with the police then you will need to contact your embassy in Cairo.

Emergency Telephone Numbers - Police 122: Ambulance 123; Fire Brigade 180.

Enemies – the walls of Luxor's temples and tombs are decorated with scenes showing the Pharaoh's supremacy over his smitten enemies but a lot of this was wishful thinking as ancient Egypt was attacked and conquered at various times by Hyksos,

Nubians, Persians, Libyans, Greeks and Romans. There are some interesting reliefs relating to the various methods of counting slain enemies in Medinet Habu.

Erotica – in ancient Egypt was as explicit as it is in the 21st century. Many ostraca found at Deir el Medina show graphic images of sexual intercourse and examples of erotic poetry have also been found there. The workmen of the village did a 10 day shift in the Valley of the Kings so many of these may have been drawn as fantasies of what they may have hoped for on return to their wives and girlfriends. Attitudes towards sex were very open with nudity and sexuality being without shame and embarrassment so they were not hidden away. There are many implied references to sex in the tombs of the Nobles through images of ducks and marshes both of which carried sexual innuendo. However, even knowing this, the erotic papyrus found in the Deir el Medina in the early 18th century, and now held in the Turin Museum (known as the Turin Erotic Papyrus), was thought to be so shocking that it was hidden away for a very long time. The papyrus shows elderly men with hugely engorged penises having sex with young women who are under the influence of the lotus narcotic. Whether this was an advertisement for a brothel or the earliest version of 'Playboy' is still a question of debate. What we think of as a quiet peaceful village could have been a hotbed of debauchery.

Esna - Esna has an attractive Greco Roman temple, dedicated to the god Khnum, but only the hypostyle hall remains. Much of the temple is still under the town and another part of it was destroyed in the 19th century when it was being used as a gunpowder store which exploded. Esna has a number of boat yards and is about 55km south of Luxor. It is easily reached by road, but the Nile cruise ships no longer moor there.

Estate Agents – there are several Estate Agencies operating in Luxor. If you are seeking a flat for long or short-term rental or wanting to buy a holiday home then it is best to go through an approved agency rather than just rely on the recommendation of a friend of a friend. Beware of ex-pats who operate in the hotels and befriend you for business. This is a quick way of saying goodbye to your money. Make sure that the Agency is actually fully registered with the Egyptian Government and has an office and not just a mobile phone and a website. Luxor4u Network Estate Agency is an Anglo/Egyptian company that is fully licensed and has a modern office close to Luxor Temple.

European Food – if you really crave fish and chips or cottage pie while on holiday then there are several restaurants catering to British tastes. Snobs and The Lantern are the main ones and there is an excellent but pricey European restaurant inside the Winter Palace Hotel. JJs at Karnak has a fish and chips take-away service.

Evenings – are short in Luxor as there is little twilight time making the time span between light and darkness very short. Mosquitoes are more active in the cool of the evening than during the day so use repellent if you are venturing near the river around sunset.

Excavations – are on-going around the tombs and many of the monuments. At present (2013) major excavations are in progress in the South Assasif area of tombs and in the area of Amenhotep's Temple.

Excuse Me – if you wish to attract someone's attention then it is polite to say 'min fadlak' – 'excuse me.'

Expats – in general the expat groups in Luxor are neither more nor less dysfunctional than anywhere else in the world. There is a large predominantly female expat population in Luxor, with British, Dutch, Danish and French making up the majority. The most contented expats appear to be those who have fully accepted the Egyptian culture and lifestyle and have the funds to live comfortably. The least content appear to be those who are living hand to mouth and are constantly worried about making ends meet. The average expat stay in Luxor is about three years before they return to their home countries. Living in Luxor can be idyllic for those with an interest in Egyptology but it is vital to be financially independent as Work Permits are very hard to get. The same warnings that apply to Egyptian-led scams also apply to ex-pats, so be careful as their honesty cannot be guaranteed and some are overly fond of venting their emotions and animosities on Facebook and open forums. (See Business Wives)

Felucca on the Nile

F

Faience - Furniture

Faience – you may see reference to scarabs, shabti and some jewellery being made of faience. Faience is sintered-quartz glazed pottery which is coloured with copper pigments to give it a blue-green colour. It is not clay based but is made from crushed quartz and has a very high lustre. It has been known in Egypt since around 4,000 BCE.

Fakka – is Arabic for 'change' or 'remainder'. If change is not offered after a transaction then hold out your hand and say 'fakka low samaht'. 'Remainder if you please.'

Falafel – is a favourite cheap local street food. It is high in protein and is made of deep fried, breadcrumb-coated, ground chick peas. It is often served by street vendors in a pocket of pitta bread with salad and pickles and tastes good. It is safe to buy from Luxor's street vendors as it will be freshly fried but have a look at the oil it is going to be fried in and make sure it is light and clean. If the oil is dark brown and old then it will leave the falafel with a bad taste.

Fanous - during Ramadan, lamps and strings of coloured lights are hung from balconies in a similar fashion to Christmas decorations in Europe. In addition, brightly coloured lanterns are hung from any available vantage point. A lamp with coloured panes is called a fanous and purpose made ones can be bought in the shops but children also make them out of cardboard and coloured cellophane.

Fauna – there were around a hundred types of wild mammals in Egypt but sadly the majority of them have been hunted to extinction. The most abundant mammals now are house mice, black and brown rats and bats. Fortunately foxes are still to be seen in Luxor. There are reports of wolves but these are mainly exaggerated as there have been no verified sighting and the animal is probably extinct in Egypt.

Fayrouz – Fayrouz is a residential area favoured by Europeans and lies at the back of the International Hospital between Television Street and Medina Street.

Fayrouz Hotel – is a pleasant west bank hotel with an excellent garden restaurant. It is situated in Gezera village and not on the Ramla.

Faxes – it is not generally easy to send or receive faxes in Luxor even if you have a fax machine but several big hotels have Business Centres that can offer the service. An alternative is to go to one of the shops that offer telephone services (there is one in Medina Street) and send the fax from there or get the fax number from them and pass it on to whoever needs to send you a fax. If the fax is not being sent immediately, leave a mobile number so that they can ring you when it arrives.

Feddan – is a land measure that was originally based on the ploughing capabilities of yoked oxen. It covers 4,200 square meters and is made up of 24 kirats.

Felaheen – refers to 'peasant farmers' and is a term applied to 60% of Egypt's rural population who still live in mud-brick houses like their ancestors did. The percentage was much higher early in the last century before there was a mass influx into the towns and in Upper Egypt it is still much higher than the national average. Poverty among the fellaheen of Luxor is endemic and illiteracy is still very high.

Felous – is Arabic for 'money'.

Felucca – is a Nile sailing boat with a single lateen sail. Day trips can be arranged and being on the river at sunset is a delight (but spray liberally with insect repellent as the mosquitoes are vicious). It is not possible to sail from Luxor to Aswan because, apart from fighting against the current, for safety reasons feluccas do not go beyond the town's outer limits but it is possible to sail from Aswan to Esna and then get a taxi back to Luxor from there.

Ferry - the ferry runs 24 hours a day for 7 days each week. Because of the river's strong current they travel in a backwards 'S' shape. During the daytime hours there are three boats taking passengers backwards and forwards; one on each side of the river and one moving across the water. They leave about every 15 – 20 minutes. The tourist fee for crossing the river is 1 LE. At night there are only 2 boats running and it can take a long time before the boat leaves the dock.

Fertility – in ancient Egypt pleas were made to the gods for fertility in women and for fertility of the land. The fertility of the land was essential to feed the people and was totally governed by the inundation of the Nile and the capriciousness of the gods so elaborate rituals were devised, such as the Opet Festival in Luxor, to keep the gods content and ensure that the annual flood was sufficient to replenish the land. Children were prized and fertile women had a higher status than barren ones so equally elaborate rituals were used to ensure the conception of children. There are phallic images of the god Min on the walls of most of Luxor's temples. In modern Luxor, fertility is still very important and wives are often expected to become pregnant in the first year of marriage, with the threat of divorce for those who do not conceive and are assumed to be barren.

Festivals – Egypt appears to have an abundance of festivals and national holidays but the main Muslim festivals are Eid el Fitr, Eid al Adha and the Birthday of Mohammed. Coptic festivals include Christmas, Easter, New Year and the Feast of St. George. Each year there are several memorial festivals with displays of horsemanship on the west bank and the Abu el Haggag festival on the east bank.

Figs – are known as 'teen' and are grown locally. They are small and sweet and can be found on most market stalls. The art is to catch them at their best when they are getting soft but have not yet split open.

Film Festivals – Luxor has recently hosted both African and European Film Festivals which have proved successful and are likely to be repeated. Many of the films were shown in the Culture Centre on the Movenpick Road.

Fire Station – there are fire stations on both sides of the river. The main fire station on the East Bank is in Medina Street and on the West Bank there is a smaller one on the main road heading north just beyond the crossroads where the traffic police are based. The emergency number for the Fire Brigade is 180.

Fish – the most prolific fresh-water fish is the Nile Perch which can grow to enormous size in Lake Nasser. Most of the fish ('samak') in the markets is from the Red Sea and is brought in from Hurghada but the markets also provide an outlet for local fishermen. There is usually a 'fish cleaning man' sitting close to the fishmonger in the market who will descale, clean and fillet your fish for a few Egyptian pounds. Frozen fish in the supermarkets is usually Sea Bass and is imported.

Fish Restaurants – you can get fish and chips in any of the European style restaurants but do not expect Cod or Haddock as they are not available. There are fish restaurants on both sides of the river but Egyptians use a lot of salt in their cooking and so it is best to ask them to reduce this to a minimum to make the fish more to European taste.

Fishing – there are fishing boats on the river in the early morning and in the late afternoon using nets and not rods although rod fishermen can sometimes be seen at the ferry points. Both throw nets and drift nets are used.

Fizzy Drinks – in bottles are made for the Egyptian market and tend to be very sweet but Coke, Sprite, 7Up, Fanta, etc. in cans are the same as bought in Europe. Prices of cans tend to vary widely. In a shop, a can may cost you around 3 LE and in a coffee shop it will cost 5 LE or 6 LE but in the hotels you can at least double that amount.

Flag – the Egyptian flag has black, red and white horizontal stripes with a golden eagle centred in the central white stripe.

Flats – ('shagga') there are literally thousands of unfinished flats in Luxor. Locals build with an eye to the future regardless of the present need. Due to the lack of policing and government laxity following the revolution, a building craze gripped Egypt and a structure appears to have been erected on every available piece of land in Luxor. Many of these flats have been built in anticipation of sons' marriages and will be finished as and when needed for a son and his new wife. Others have been built in speculation of an improved tourist trade. Flats can be rented for holiday accommodation and give a freedom that is not possible in hotels.

Flies – unfortunately Egypt has more than its fair share of flies ('deban') and they can be persistent and pesky as they buzz around you attracted by the moisture on your skin. Keep a can of fly spray in your room. You can get a can at any pharmacy or supermarket and it will deal with the mosquitoes as well as the flies. Some of the flies bite but insect repellent can keep them at bay.

Flights – several airlines have direct flights into Luxor from the UK but these are mainly charter flights and there are rules in force over how charter flights can be used. From the UK, Thomson and Monarch have charter flights to Luxor on Mondays and Wednesdays. Egypt Air and easyJet have scheduled flights into Luxor but the frequency of the easyJet flights is determined by demand. There are frequent Egypt Air connecting flights into Luxor from Cairo.

Flooding – it is hard to imagine flooding in Luxor with its low rainfall and control of the Nile through the Aswan Dam but devastating floods following torrential rain do occur every decade or so and lead to loss of life and great hardship when mud brick houses collapse. There are now storm drains on the west bank that will help to alleviate the problem there but without street drainage flooding still occurs.

Flora – sadly, the wonderful lotus flower that tops many of the columns in Luxor's temples no longer grows in Luxor even though it was the emblematic plant of Upper Egypt. The papyrus reed, from which the ancient scrolls were made and which was the emblematic plant of Lower Egypt, has also been lost although it is now grown commercially in the delta area. Date Palms proliferate and bougainvillea and hibiscus can be found flowering everywhere.

FMG – (female genital mutilation) is unfortunately part of Upper Egypt's culture. It has little to do with religion as it is practiced by all faiths. Statistics show that approximately 95% of Egyptian women and girls in Luxor have been 'cut', which involves the complete removal of the clitoris. The practice was outlawed some time ago after several girls bled to death but this had little impact on its occurrence and another girl died during the procedure in June 2013. Several excuses have put forward that are supposed to make this a necessity. Not only men support it but also women who had it done to them as children and who have never known anything different. Among the excuses are:- women who have not had it done 'have trouble walking' or 'might want sex all the time like European women do'; and also because 'it is for cleanliness', 'daughters might not stay pure' or 'men will not marry women who have not been cut'. It is done for control and women support it because some men actually will not marry a woman who has not been cut and they fear that their daughters might later be considered unsuitable as brides. As many medical professionals now decline to perform the illegal operation it is sometimes done by 'granny' on the kitchen floor using a razor blade. Scarring and infection are common.

Football – Egyptians are as obsessed with football as any European nation and, when there is a match involving the national team, groups gather around any available television. There is a football ground behind the playground off Medina Street and a youth football ground at the Nasser Club behind the government offices on the Movenpick Road. Egypt is the most successful nation in the Africa Cup of Nations having won the contest seven times. Battling football fans caused problems recently leading to many deaths in Port Said.

Footwear – the standard indoor footwear for Egyptians is flip-flops known as 'ship ships' which are ideal for wearing around the pool. In the street, sandals are the norm. However, if you are looking at the monuments you could be moving over rough ground and climbing up and down very narrow steep stairs so more substantial footwear is needed.

Forty Supermarket – is situated in Hospital Street and has a wide range of products. It also stocks fresh fruit and vegetables.

Foul – ('fool') is the Arabic name for fava beans and is a favourite breakfast dish. In central Luxor, instant makeshift pavement cafes appear after dawn selling beans to people on their way to work.

Foxes – seeing foxes leaving the fields at sunset on the west bank is sheer delight. They are small and timid with a white flash at the end of their tails. There are several species of fox in Egypt but the one commonly seen around Luxor is the Red (or Nile) Fox. Desert foxes (Fennec & Ruppell's Sand Foxes) have been sighted near Dendera but usually stay well out in the desert. Egyptians tend to be afraid of foxes.

Frogs – in spring the sound of croaking frogs dominates the night air when you are close to the Nile. Frogs were the second biblical plague to befall Egypt.

Fruit - a great deal of the fruit on sale in the markets is grown locally. Most of it is seasonal. Guava looks like a pear and has pink or white flesh (the pink is more succulent). Local grapes are green and of two basic varieties; small and extra sweet and large and juicy. Locally grown oranges and tangerines are available and so are lemons. Water melons are huge and delicious and mangos are sublime. Local dates, figs and peaches are available in season. Bananas are small and sweet. Egyptian strawberries are available in the winter months and have an intense flavour.

Funerals – Muslim funerals usually take place within 24 hours of a death. The first notification of a death is the loud trilling of family and neighbours. On the west bank a service car will sometimes tour the streets advising people of the death through loud speakers. Women, dressed head to toe in black, will descend on the home of the deceased and sit in the street for up to five days of mourning. Only men attend the actual funeral and the body is carried through the streets on a bier to the mosque and then carried on to the cemetery. Strangers will help carry the bier as there is kudos in assisting. The body is then buried lying full length facing Mecca in a chamber which is then bricked up and sealed.

Funerary Processes – in ancient times funerary processes were designed to reunite the Ka which left the body on death, to the Ba which remained with it. For eternal life the Ba had to be released so that the Ka and the Ba could fly away from the tomb together each day with the Ba returning to the body again each night. Mummification was designed to preserve the body from decay so that it could be used on this daily journey. (See Mummification.)

Furniture - if you are thinking of settling in Luxor and wish to buy furniture then it is worthwhile having it made to order as Egyptian furniture has a tendency to be straight backed, hard and uncomfortable. Just bring a catalogue with you and the furniture makers will copy the item to your specification. There are several furniture shops in Luxor mainly centred around Medina Street but if you wish to have furniture made then it is more economical to approach the makers directly. The furniture making area can be found along the road which runs with a right-hand turn off the first roundabout on Temple Karnak Street in the Karnak direction.

The Golden Mask of Tutankhamun

G

Gabal – Gymnasiums

Gabal – is Arabic for 'mountain'. The Theban Hills are not really high enough to be called mountains but that is how the Qurn is referred to by locals.

Gaddis Hotel – is a family owned 3* tourist hotel with a swimming pool at the Movenpick Road end of Khaled Ibn el Walid Street. There are karaoke nights and special events at Christmas and New Year. It is also where the office of Mr. Ehab Gaddis can be found. Mr Gaddis was the British Honorary Consul for many years and still acts in the role but, due to complications with Egyptian law, does so without the title.

Gaddis Shop – the Gaddis shop on the Corniche is very long established and sells a wide range of tourist items plus atmospheric prints of photographs that were taken in the late nineteenth century and early twentieth century by members of the Gaddis family.

Gamal – is Arabic for a 'camel'. There are however even more Arabic words for camels as there are Inuit words to describe snow.

Garages – there are several large fuel-dispensing garages on the edges of Luxor and on the west bank. However, there are frequent fuel shortages which can lead to long queues. There are also numerous small vehicle repair shops like the one about halfway down Television Street that has a full-size water-filled bath outside for testing tyres and inner tubes. Most are kept busy bashing out the dents that all too frequently occur in traffic accidents.

Garlic – (toom) is very important in Egyptian cooking and is sold in the markets in kilograms instead of small bunches as in Europe.

Gas – is another name for diesel and suffers the same shortages as benzene. Most mini buses and trucks run off diesel. Very long queues can form at garages and tempers can get frayed.

Gay Visitors - homosexuality may be acknowledged behind closed doors but there is no open acceptance of it as there is in western cultures. Consequently many gay Egyptians consider themselves to be persecuted. However, there is a gay trade carried on along the Corniche after dark and in some coffee shops. Many male tourists, particularly those travelling alone, may find themselves harassed and have to fend off the unwanted attention of rent boys. Gay visitors need to be aware that homosexuality is frowned upon by most Egyptians and any open display of it may well cause 'difficulties' and you would receive little sympathy from the law.

Gebel el Silsila – lies between Luxor and Aswan (65 km north of Aswan) in a place where the river narrows on both sides. It was used as a quarry site in ancient times and stone from there was used extensively by Akhenaten in Luxor and Tel el Armana; most of the stone for the west bank temples came from there. On the western side of the river are rock cut shrines for Horemheb, Seti I, Ramses II and Merenptah and there is also a chapel built by Horemheb that shows his military successes.

Geckos – are unique among lizards in that they vocalise socially with other geckos. They do not have eyelids but have a membrane covering their eyes which they lick to keep them moist and they have suckered feet which allows them to climb walls with ease. They live on insects and mosquitoes which makes them welcome house guests. (See Chit Chats.)

Gellabyia – is a long sleeved cotton housedress worn by women. Men also wear gellabyias but they are of a different design and have pockets at each side and sometimes have a breast pocket. Men's gellabyias can have short sleeves but women never bare their arms. There are some lovely embroidered gellabyias in the souk with prices varying from 35 LE–150 LE depending on style and quality.

Genesis Bar – is a restaurant/bar in Karnak village with joint Egyptian and Ukrainian ownership. It has an extensive menu of freshly cooked food and a flat screen TV for watching football. The décor can only be described as 'different', and with a swimming pool behind the bar and a pet ostrich, it is well worth a visit!

Gezera - Gezera is simply Arabic for 'island' so there are a lot of places called Gezera around Luxor. However, the ones that are usually referred to are (1) the village area close to the west bank ferry terminal and (2) the east bank area on the bridge side of Awamia - but there are many more to the north and the south of Luxor.

Gezera Gardens Hotel – is situated on the Ramla area of the west bank close to the ferry. The hotel offers self-catering flats as well as the usual hotel rooms. There is a swimming pool, restaurant and bar. The pool is open to non-residents for a small fee.

Giardia – is a protozoan parasite that infests the gut and leads to giardisis. It is picked up through bad hygiene or infected water. Its symptoms are extremely foul flatulence, diarrhoea and breath that smells of bad eggs. It can be cured with a single dose of Flagyl that can be bought from any pharmacy.

Gifts – many Egyptians have an alarming tendency to ask you what the gift you have just given them cost. In Europe this is seen as rude but in Egypt appears to be acceptable and allows them to brag to their friends. If you are asked to eat with a family you may wish to take a gift with you. Buying cakes, sweets or biscuits is recommended but do not expect them to be opened, shared and eaten while you are there. They will be eaten later. (See Presents.)

Gigolo – whether it is in Egypt, Turkey, Gambia, Dominican Republic, Kenya or anywhere there is poverty coupled with tourists and a surfeit of good-looking men, there will be a gigolo problem. 'Lonely hearts' is global business and in Luxor it is a big source of income which causes a lot of heartache for many tourists each year when they fall in love and then realise that they have been 'conned'. Most victims will have handed over money for ill-conceived ventures and some will have sold their houses in Europe to fund a non-existent new life. This is only a reflection on a certain element of society as most Egyptian men are honest and in monogamous relationships. As a warning, if a relationship appears to be too good to be true then think carefully as it actually will be too good to be true. It is not within the Egyptian culture for a man to marry a woman who is many years his senior and may be beyond child bearing age. Sadly, when the situation becomes evident, many of the women feel betrayed and become bitter if they did not leave themselves a financial escape route. Trying to get your money back is like chasing shadows and spending money on lengthy court cases is a waste of time as the police have hundreds of files which are all the same but with different names on them. You may not be able to protect your heart but you can protect your finances. (See Business Wives.)

Glottal Stop – in Arabic there is a glottal stop between some vowels that inserts a small cough like sound and splits the vowel into two syllables instead of one. It is shown in phonetic translations as an apostrophe but in Luxor this 'stop' is filled with a positive 'g' sound.

Goats – it is not unusual to see flocks of sheep and goats on the streets of Luxor or 'corralled' on roof tops. They are brought along the streets in the early morning by their herder who tears open the rubbish bags for them to eat the waste food. Goat meat is more strongly flavoured than lamb (lahma daani) but is often labelled as 'lamb' in local restaurants and tastes good. Both sheep and goats are often shaggy and it can sometimes be hard to differentiate between them so simply look at their tails. Goats' tails point upwards and sheep's tails point downwards.

Gods – there are literally hundreds of gods in Egyptian mythologies but they were mainly worshipped on a regional or local basis. Although there is a crossover with the major gods, the gods of the north were not always worshipped in the south. Luxor had its own favourite gods the principal of which was Amun.

Gold – ('dahab') Luxor and gold have always been linked. Luxor's most famous pieces of gold are Tutankhamun's mask and coffin now in Cairo Museum. There are many gold shops in Luxor and these are not devoted to the tourist trade as is it traditional for brides to be presented with gold jewellery at their wedding. The amount of gold given will depend on the wealth of the groom and the desirability of the bride and will be stated in the marriage contract. This gold then belongs to the bride even if there is a later divorce. Muslim men were expressly forbidden to wear gold by the prophet Mohammed (pbuh). Now tourists buy gold jewellery in the form of sphinxes and scarabs to remind them of their holiday. Egypt is still a gold producer with its largest mine being in the south western desert. The same warnings apply to buying gold that apply to everything else (buyer beware) and remember that if you are in a gold shop with a guide then he/she may be in line to receive 50% of the amount that you spend.

Golf – there is an 18-hole golf course in Luxor called the Royal Valley. It is situated several kms from the airport. There is a Nubian style Club House and a shop. There is a range of tees at each station to reflect the expertise of the golfer.

Good Samaritans – is a small well supported Coptic charity which runs a home for disabled children and elderly adults in a rambling house at the rear of the Santa Maria Cathedral.

Governor – Luxor Governorate was created in December 2009 as the 29th Governorate in Egypt. There have been several different Governors since 2011 which has exacerbated an already unsettled situation.

Grapes – locally grown grapes (known as 'anab') can be found on all the market stalls and are very inexpensive when in season. There are two types generally on offer both of which are green; black grapes are usually imported and relatively expensive. Of the local grapes, the sweetest are the very small ones that grow in tight bunches.

Green Bee Eaters – are very attractive birds and can be seen sitting on the telephone wires on the west bank as they rest during their migratory journey south.

Greetings – the formal greeting is 'Salaam alykum' (peace be with you). The response is 'Wa alykum as salaam' but which is generally shortened to 'alykum salaam'. The informal equivalent of 'Hi' is 'ahlan'. Good morning is "Sabah el kheir'.

Guide Books – there are some excellent detailed Guide Books specifically about Luxor and its monuments, one of the best of which is by Kent Weeks. The Lonely Planet Guide to Egypt is useful as a general guide to the area. If you are only coming to Upper Egypt then detach that section and leave the rest behind.

Gymnasiums – most of the upmarket hotels have gym facilities and allow non-residents access for a fairly hefty fee. There is a well- established gym on the east bank called Star Gym off Medina Street on the opposite side of the road to Omar Market and a new gym is opening on the west bank on the main road close to Qurna Hospital.

The Goddess Hathor – Deir el Bahri

H
Habibi - Hypostyle

Habibi – is a term of affection used between friends of both sexes. It is the same as saying 'sweetheart', 'darling' or 'my love'. Men are more likely to call their male friends Habibi than their female ones as addressing a women in this way could be interpreted as being over-familiar. An Egyptian man might call his girlfriend Habibti but this word is not used if referring to merely a female acquaintance.

Haggling – is a national pastime and in the souks haggling is expected of you. Prior to giving you a price for something, a stall-holder may ask you where you are from. This is not from interest in you but is a guide to what price he should quote as some nationalities are more likely to bargain than others. The British are not natural hagglers and walk away rather than argue the price. In most cases you can offer one third of the asking price and expect to pay half.

Hairdressers – several beauty parlours have recently opened in Luxor offering spa treatments and hairdressing the newest of which is at the Television Street end of Hospital Street. These are aimed at the local market and not at tourists but offer the usual range of services. There are also several expat hairdressers living in Luxor who cut and style hair but they do not have their own salons and either visit or work from home.

Hajj – relates to the obligatory pilgrimage to Mecca that is one of the five pillars of Islam. The same word also used as an honorific title when addressing older men.

Halal – means 'permissible' and applies to many aspects of daily life that are deemed 'good' but is mainly applied to food which should be prepared in a way that is permissible in Islam.

Halas – means 'done', 'finish' or 'stop'. If you are being hassled beyond endurance and the polite 'la shokran' (no thank you) statement is having no effect then hold your hand up in front of you with your palm outwards and in a very firm voice say 'Halas'. The hassler will then know that you mean it and should leave you alone.

Hantour – the term hantour is applied to the converted flat-back trucks that are used as passenger vehicles in an around the villages (these are slowly being replaced with mini-buses), the horse drawn carts known as calleches and also the curtained box-like passenger contraption that is carried by camels.

Haram – means 'sinful' and is applied to various aspects of daily life such as idolatry and fornication but is mainly applied to certain food (carrion, blood and swine flesh) and to alcohol forbidden to Muslims by the Qur'an. Haram acts are supposedly recorded by an angel sitting on the left shoulder.

Harami – is a 'criminal' – someone who has indulged in acts that are haram.

Harem – there are three kinds of harem that relate to Luxor. The first is the 'women's quarters' of the Pharaohs' palaces. These were not just inhabited by a Pharaoh's wives but by mothers, sisters, daughters, aunts and all female relatives that lived in the palace. Even in monogamous less rich households there could be a room that was set aside purely for the use of women. Harems persisted in the ruling elite of Egypt into the 20th Century. The second kind of harem is the congregation of virgin priestesses that served Amun under the direction of 'God's Wife'. Luxor temple was known as the 'Harem of the South' as the god Amun met his wife Mut there for their annual honeymoon during the Opet Festival. The third kind of harem is that gathered by the more successful gigolos who are known to have several European Business Wives on the go at any one time, all of whom are ignorant of each other's existence. Juggling their visits to Luxor then becomes an art form.

Hathor – is the Egyptian goddess dedicated to love, joy and motherhood. She is often depicted as having the ears of a cow and her headdress shows cow horns holding the sun. She is sometimes shown as suckling Horus. There is a chapel to her in

Deir el Bahri (Hatshepsut's Temple) and her image is used to cap the columns in the temple which is dedicated to her at Deir el Medina (Workers' Village) and the Opet Temple at Karnak. She is described as both the wife and the daughter of the god Ra. She was greatly venerated by the Ptolemies who dedicated a magnificent temple to her at Dendera.

Hatshepsut – was not Egypt's first female ruler but she was the first to hold the position in her own right as Pharaoh. In her images, she wears a man's beard which was the expected norm for images of Pharaohs at that time. She was a prolific builder and her temple (see Deir el Bahri) in the west bank necropolis is one of the oldest and is certainly worth visiting. There has been extensive renovation of the temple in recent years which has gone way beyond preservation but it is a fascinating place and is very different in style from the later temples. There is also a Red Chapel (made of red quartzite) to her at Karnak. The chapel had been dismantled in ancient times and used as infill on one of the later pylons but has been reconstructed in the open air museum. Recently, her White Chapel has also been reconstructed in the open air museum. Her mummy was 'discovered' in 2007 when a seemingly insignificant mummy from KV60 was, by matching a molar tooth that was known to be hers with a gap in the mummy's dentures, formally identified as that of the great queen. Her mummy is being restored in Cairo and will, presumably, join her illustrious forbears and descendants in the Royal Mummies Room in the Cairo Museum in due course. (See Royal Mummies and Tutmosis III.)

Health – these is no reason why you should have any health problems in Egypt although many visitors report attacks of Pharaoh's Revenge. One of the main sources of gastric infection in Luxor is from rice ('ruz'). Choose chips (French fries) instead as they are freshly cooked and the rice base could actually be days old. Other problems usually stem from dehydration so drink a lot (though not alcohol which itself exacerbates dehydration!). If you leave it until you are thirsty it is already too late.

Health Scares – during the SARS panic, all visitors arriving at Luxor airport had their temperature taken and had to fill in a contact form even though there were no reported SARS cases in Egypt. If there is a health scare about anything when you are visiting Luxor then be prepared for delays at the airport. When the bird flu panic hit Egypt all the chickens were culled and the pelicans at the Sheraton Hotel were killed. It was the same with swine flu. Then all the pigs in Egypt were slaughtered. Over-reaction is the norm.

Henna – is used for hair colouring and for the wonderful temporary tattoos that women sometimes have on their hands and feet before a wedding or family celebration. The leaves of the plant will dye skin only if they are broken up so that the dyes can be released and the effect is temporary. Henna grows easily in Egypt and is found in many gardens. Its flowers are highly scented. Some skin is very sensitive to henna and should be tested before applying it to a large area.

Hepatitis – comes in three forms (A, B and C); all are significant in Luxor. Hep A can be caused by something you might eat or drink or by sex with an infected person but it is no more of a problem in Egypt than it is elsewhere and although the initial symptoms are severe, they do fade. In 2004 there was a major outbreak in Hurghada involving British tourists and this was traced back to orange juice that had been unhygienically prepared. Hep B is a bigger problem but you can be immunised against it. In Egypt, the main causes have been found to be sexual intercourse, barber shop cuts and injecting drug use (diabetes and addiction). Many of the cases found in Egyptian women were passed to them by their new spouses through first-time wedding-night sex, which, because of FMG scarring, can cause vaginal tearing. Pre-marriage checks are now advised but few will be done. Vaccines are available for Hep A and Hep B. The most dangerous form is Hep C which has no cure. Egypt has the highest Hep C rate in the world with nearly 15% of the adult population testing positive. The causes are the same as those given for other Hepatitis strains but Hep C is blood to blood only and there is still no known cure so be careful with cuts and casual sex as the liver damage Hep C causes can prove fatal.

Herbs – bunches of a variety of fresh herbs can be bought for between 50 piastras and 1 LE in the local markets. Coriander and mint are the most commonly found.

Heritage Centre – used to be called the Susan Mubarak Heritage Centre until the fall of the Mubarak regime. The Centre is an imposing white building on the road to Karnak Temple. It has exhibitions, hosts conferences and has a library.

Herodotus – was a Greek historian from the 5th century BCE who travelled widely and visited Luxor; writing extensively about daily life, the priesthood and flora and fauna of the region. One of his life-style observations concerned embalming women. The bodies of the wives of prominent men were not taken to the embalmers until they had been dead for several days. This was to preserve the dignity of the women and to stop their bodies being 'abused' by over-eager embalmers.

Herons – there are several species of herons to be found in Egypt especially during the winter migration when they rest on the islands that form in the Nile when the water level is low. Egrets are there all year and roost in the trees as a colony. The sacred ibis have sadly gone but grey herons boost their numbers for part of the year.

Hieroglyph – the word hieroglyph derives from the Greek words for 'sacred writing'. It is the pictorial written language of the ancient Egyptians. The walls of the temples and tombs are covered with hieroglyphs which relate the Pharaoh's exploits or give the instructions from the Book of the Dead on how to enter and travel through the Underworld. The meaning of the language is known through the deciphering of the Rosetta Stone (held in the British Museum) but what the language sounded like is totally unknown, although as the Coptic alphabet is based on the Ancient Egyptian language, it might have sounded similar.

Hijab – is the head covering worn by Muslim women. It takes many forms and some are decorative. There are transient fashions in how it is worn and there is constant debate over whether wearing the hijab is mandatory or discretionary. Hijabs do not cover the face.

Hilton Hotel – has a genuine 5* rating, is situated in Karnak and has recently been totally renovated.

Homosexuality – is considered a perversion in Egypt and, although it happens behind closed doors, it is not openly accepted. However, except for indecency, there appears to be no direct law against it. Publicly displayed acts of affection between men and women are discouraged but openly shown affection between friends of the same sex is not unusual. Many Egyptian men will link arms and hold hands in the street with other men; this is a display of affection for friends and does not indicate that they are gay.

Honour Killings – sadly there is a complete double standard between men and women over morality and honour killings of women are not uncommon. While men can more or less do as they please, if a woman is unfaithful, or if a girl becomes pregnant (even as a result of incest), then she may be considered to have brought dishonour on the family. Self-righteous family members can then feel that they are justified in taking her life. It is against the law but the courts have been accused of occasionally giving overly lenient sentences even when guilt is admitted. In June 2013 three women were deliberately drowned in the Nile when a family thought it had been disgraced through infidelity.

Hoopoes – are also known as Hod Hod birds and, due to their crests, are the Mohicans of the bird world. They are mainly pink and have black and white striped wings. They can be seen on both sides of the river. They were considered sacred in ancient Egypt and can be found in the wall paintings of several tombs. Their nests are scruffy and extremely smelly.

Horses – many, but not all, of the carriage horses seen in Luxor are maltreated and underfed which is surprising as people are dependent upon them for their livelihood. It is a strange mind set. However, there are well kept horses at the riding stables close to the west bank ferry. There are also horses that are maintained in peak condition and are ridden by their owners with pride at various festivals. The overall condition of many of the calleche horses has improved due to the care offered by ACE and the Brooke Clinic.

Horus – is a sky god and is the son of the god Osiris and his sister/wife Isis. Horus is multi-faceted, encompasses several forms and performs several roles. He is usually shown having a hawk's head with a crown to show that he rules all of Egypt but in another form is shown with the sun as his headdress. The eye of Horus is seen as a symbol of protection. There was an epic battle between Horus and Seth in defence of his father Osiris with neither god being the overall victor and both suffering injuries. Horus's four sons are seen protecting the dead in several tombs. The Pharaoh was seen as the earthly manifestation of Horus and bore a 'Horus' name. (See Sons of Horus.)

Horus Temple – the main Horus temple is Ptolemaic and is in Edfu which is to the south of Luxor. It was uncovered in the 1860s and is one of the most intact temples in Egypt. As the temple was buried it is below the level of the town. The cruise boats stop there so that passengers can see the temple but it can easily be reached by road from Luxor.

Hospital Street – is so called because it runs alongside the International Hospital between Television Street and Medina Street.

Hospitals – most injuries and illnesses are dealt with in the large International Hospital in Television Street but there is now a new private hospital in St. Joseph's Street which has good recommendations. There are several 'local' hospitals in Luxor but they do not normally accept European patients or admit European visitors.

Humour - Egyptians have a great sense of humour and often play jokes on each other. They are very fond of slap-stick comedy films and television programmes.

Hurghada – is often chosen for the second week of a holiday with a Nile cruise taking up the first week. The only purpose for the existence of this elongated town is as a tourist resort which is greatly favoured by Germans and Russians. It is also the busiest Red Sea resort and diving centre after Sharm el Sheikh. However, there is still some charm in the downtown area. There was a major construction boom in the early 2000's which ground to a halt following the 2008 world recession and the 2011 revolution. Vast areas of the town now consist of unfinished residential developments and makes Hurghada look like a 10 mile long building site. The journey from Luxor by car takes about 4 hours and there is also a regular bus service.

Hypochondria – in Egypt is a national pastime where every ache, pain and scratch calls for a visit to a doctor and necessitates an injection of some kind. Self-medication is rife and if one set of medicines does not seem to work then often another set is bought and taken alongside the first set. There is an extraordinary fear of bird flu, swine flu, SARS and every health panic that reaches the news.

Hypostyle – many of Luxor's temples have hypostyle halls. The term refers to a roof that is supported by a series of columns. The most famous hypostyle hall is the one at Karnak which represents the world emerging from the primeval swamp. Many mosques follow the same pattern of having a large space with a roof that is supported by ornate columns.

The Egret is Often Mistaken for the Sacred Ibis

I
Ibis – Itching

Ibis – the African Sacred Ibis was worshipped by the ancient Egyptians but was sadly slaughtered and mummified out of existence. Millions of mummified birds have been found in subterranean passages as offerings to the gods, particularly to Thoth who is shown with the head of an Ibis. Its cousin, the glossy ibis, is still to be found around Luxor but the birds that some people think of as being sacred ibis are in fact egrets. Attempts were being made to reintroduce it in Egypt but these were shelved following the 2011 revolution.

Ice – the ice you have in your drinks in Luxor will be made from tap water but as the water is potable you will not be in any danger of contracting any diseases through it.

Iftar – is the ceremonial breaking of the fast at sunset during Ramadan. It is often done as a community with tables set out in the street so that people can break their fast together. Usually, dates are eaten first which follows the tradition set by Mohammed (pbuh) who broke his own fast in this way. During Ramadan the streets are totally deserted at this time and it is almost impossible to get transport or any kind of service.

Illuminations – a great deal of work has been done in recent years on illuminating the Theban Hills and the temples on both sides of the river. The Theban Hills now make a spectacular night-time sight of shadow and light when viewed from the east bank. Work has also been done in adding pleasant lighting to the newly pedestrianised area of the Corniche to the north of the El Luxor (Etap) Hotel. Early in 2013 part of the restored Avenue of Sphinxes was attractively floodlit. Luxor Temple is floodlit at night and open to visitors. In the summer, this is the best time to visit this temple. (See Sound and Light.)

Imam – is a leader of the local Muslim community through the mosque.

Imshi – means 'go away' and is usually said to children. Adult males who are told to 'Imshi' often get annoyed and may reply 'how dare you tell me to go away in my own country.'

Insha Allah – is frequently added to the end of a sentence and simply means 'God willing' but is often used as a way of not answering simple questions.

International Airports– in Upper Egypt, Luxor, Aswan, and Hurghada have international airports. Luxor's airport is situated approximately 7 km from the town. Prices for coffee and snacks are comparative to Heathrow airport rather than the local prices. A small cup of coffee in a cardboard cup costs in excess of £2 GBP and a packet of crisps costs around £1.50 GBP. The recommendation is to bring your own as you can take fluids as far as the departure gates. The customs staff on arrival can be draconian with women travelling alone and anyone they see as a frequent visitor so be prepared to have your bags searched and to be asked how many mobile phones, 'electroniques' or medicines you have hidden in your bags. There can also be bag searches when you are leaving if the authorities think that you may have hidden antiquities. There are duty free shops in both the Arrivals and Departure areas.

International Hospital – is on Television Street but the entrance used by most people is at the back of the Hospital. Reports on treatment are both good and bad. Charges vary depending on residency and, if you are not insured, there is an insistence on someone accepting the cost of treatment before you are admitted for a hospital stay. Their out-patients department offers help to all and the costs are not high and could be your first port of call if you are taken ill.

Internet Cafes – there are many low cost Internet Cafes in Luxor but they are not real cafes offering drinks, just computer use. Many of them have key loggers installed so do not use them for sensitive information. Prices range from 2 LE to 10 LE per hour. Hotels charge a great deal more for computer use but may offer more security. One recommended is the 'Friends' Internet Café off Salah el Din Square.

Inundation – Upper Egypt was totally dependent on the inundation (flooding of the Nile) but now this is controlled by the Aswan dam. The inundation was celebrated through the Opet Festival and the flooding brought fertile Nile silt onto the land which is sadly now missing. Flooding does still occur but is through the heavy rainfall that occurs every decade or so. This problem is being dealt with through the installation of storm drains.

Ironing shops – in Egypt ironing clothes is mainly a man's job probably because it involves a machine. Ironing shops are found all over Luxor with a standard charge of 50 piastras for ironing any item.

Irrigation – Luxor is desert area and only supports vegetation through constant watering. This is achieved through a series of pumps on interlocking canals which feed water into channels leading to the fields. It is possible to step from lush green vegetation to desert dry earth at the edge of the irrigated area. Experiments are progressing in irrigating desert areas with waste water.

Isis – is one of the principal Egyptian gods. She is the sister/wife of Osiris and mother of Horus. She is shown with a throne hieroglyph as her headdress but is also shown wearing a solar disk mounted between cow horns which makes her easily mistaken for Hathor. Sometimes, only the image's surrounding hieroglyphs differentiate the two goddesses. Isis's most important temple is on the Island of Philae in Aswan. She is associated with motherhood and the care of children and with secrets and magic as she was able to restore Osiris's body after it was dismembered by their brother Seth. She is also known as a protector of the dead and her image frequently appears on the walls of temples and tombs alongside that of her sister Nephthys.

Isis Hotel – the Pyramisa Isis is a large 5* hotel on Khaled Ibn el Walid Street. It has a large pool and there is a resident singer most evenings.

Islam – is the main religion in Egypt with 90% of the population being Sunni Muslims. The religion is monotheistic and follows the rulings of the Koran (Quran) which were given to the prophet Mohammed (pbuh) as the direct word of God. There are five pillars of Islam: the belief in God, prayer, fasting, alms for the poor and a pilgrimage to Mecca.

Islands – ('gezera') although the Nile waters are governed by the Aswan dam, the water still rises and falls with the seasons causing islands in the river to appear and disappear. In winter the islands become green with vegetation and are inhabited by myriads of migrating birds making it ideal for bird watchers.

Issyak – asks 'how are you'; to which you could reply 'kwyis Alhamdulillah'. 'Good, thanks be to God.'

Itching – mosquito and other insect bites can cause intense irritation to those who react badly to them. Put some anti-histamine tablets and cream in your suitcase before you leave home or call in a local pharmacy and ask them what is available. Prickly heat can also be a problem. If you are prone to prickly heat cover your arms when going out in the sun.

Egyptian Jewellery

J
Jana - Juma

Jana - (or Jannah) is Arabic for 'paradise' or 'heaven'.

Jana Restaurant – is a widely recommended restaurant in Karnak close to the Hilton Hotel. It is well designed and has both indoor and open-air eating areas.

Jesus Christ - is revered as a prophet in Islam and as the son of God in the Coptic Church which makes him important across the religions in Egypt. Mary and Joseph are said to have fled to Egypt with the infant Jesus to avoid Herod's slaughter of the innocents. Egypt was the first stronghold of Christianity and may have adapted to the new religion more easily than in other places as the people were accustomed to the idea of a theological triad through Isis, Osiris and Horus, and through Amun, Mut and Khonsu. There are Christian images in the rear part of Luxor Temple (in the Festival hall of Tutmosis III).

Jewellery – the best display of ancient Egyptian jewellery is in Cairo Museum, although there are several items of the fabulous jewellery of Queen Ahhotep on display in Luxor Museum. There are numerous jewellery shops in Luxor with many items being sold by weight. Shop around before you buy anything and remember that if you were taken to the shop by a Tour Guide then he may receive a large percentage of the purchase price of any item you buy as soon as you have paid for it. The technical skill of the ancient craftsmen was superb and those skills have not been lost as it is still possible to have pieces of jewellery made to your own specification. Egyptian women have a tendency to wear items made entirely of gold instead of incorporating precious stones. Gold is still mined in Egypt.

JJs – is a European owned restaurant/bar, with live music, in a side street in Karnak. The music is superb with Col Coleman on the guitar and Axel Langer on the keyboards. They offer a wide range of beers and wines and also do a take-away service which, to the delight of expats, includes fish and chips.

Jolie Ville Hotel – used to be called the Movenpick and is a large 5* hotel with bungalow accommodation situated between Luxor town and the Nile bridge. It has recently undergone extensive renovation and extension. The 'infinity' pool is a great attraction.

Juice Bars – there are inexpensive juice bars spread throughout Luxor serving glasses of delicious freshly pressed oranges and liquidised mangos. Sugar cane is also pressed and served as a sweet sticky juice that is greatly favoured by Egyptians. A wide variety of fruit juices can be bought in cartons from any supermarket.

Juma – is the holy day of the Islamic week. It starts at sunset on Thursday and finishes at sunset on Friday. Most of the shops in Luxor will close during daylight hours on Fridays. As all Muslim men are expected to attend the mosque for midday prayers on Fridays, the calls to prayer are extended and mosques seem to vie with each other for attention.

Obelisk of Hatshepsut at Karnak Temple

K
Ka – KV5

Ka – in ancient Egypt the Ka was the vital spark that was breathed into a body at birth and left a body at death. It was not the soul but was considered part of it; a concept similar to that of the human spirit. For eternal life it was vital for the Ka and the Ba to reunite.

Kanafa – is a thin, dry wheat-based cake ingredient that is used during Ramadan. You can see it being poured and dried on large flat hot-plates in the markets. It comes in long strings but is then broken into small pieces like shredded wheat and mixed with sugar and dried fruit. After mixing, it is baked and then soaked with a sweet juice-based liquid to make a delicious cake.

Karaoke – is not to everyone's taste but there is a shortage of nightlife in Luxor. Karaoke sessions are held in the Gaddis Hotel in Khaled Ibn el Walid Street every Tuesday and Saturday night.

Karkardeh – is a delicious deep purple coloured drink made from dried Hibiscus flowers. It can be served hot or cold and is very refreshing. It is not made from the flowers of the garden shrub but from an annual plant. It is sold by weight and the price varies with the quality.

Karnak – was the name of the boat in Agatha Christie's novel 'Death on the Nile'. The MS Memnon posed as the Karnak in the 1948 film and the MS Sudan in the later film.

Karnak Temple - Karnak is not one temple but a whole complex of temples, shrines and pylons. It takes its modern name from the nearby village. The ancient Egyptians called it 'Ipet Sut'. – (Most Esteemed of Places). Much of the building currently standing was done in the New Kingdom era but building actually started in the Middle Kingdom era and continued right through and beyond Ptolemaic times. The site is dedicated to Amun and his wife Mut and their son Khonsu. It covers a vast area and only part of it is open to the public although other precincts may soon be accessible. The most famous part of the temple is the magnificent hypostyle hall which was used as a backdrop for a fight between James Bond and his adversary 'Jaws' in the 1977 film 'The Spy Who Loved Me'. It also appeared in Agatha Christie's 'Death on the Nile'. No matter how many times you visit the temple you will always see something new. Take time away from tour groups and wander around the temples at your own pace absorbing the ambience and imagining what it would have been like in its days of splendour. Admission is 65 LE and there is a further charge to enter the Open-Air Museum section.

Karnak Village –is situated about 2.5 km north of Luxor. There are several good restaurants there such as the Jana, Genesis Bar, Gerda's Garden and JJs. The Hilton Hotel which offers 5* accommodation is there and the excellent Sofitel Hotel is close by.

KFC – Kentucky Fried Chicken arrived in Luxor a few years ago and is situated at the junction of Khaled Ibn el Walid Street and the Movenpick Road. They have a home delivery service.

Khaled Ibn el Walid Street – is the road where many of the major hotels are situated and where there were plans for a new Four Seasons Hotel. It is a straight dual-carriage road that runs from the roundabout at the southern end of the Corniche through to the junction of the Movenpick Road.

Khawaj and Khawajyia – means 'foreign man' and 'foreign woman' respectively and is widely used when describing Europeans.

Khnum – is one of the earliest Egyptian gods and was worshipped as the creator of the Nile. He is shown with a ram's head and his function was to create human children from Nile clay on a potter's wheel. His image (recognisable by the horizontal spiralling horns) can be seen in the 'birth scenes' at

Luxor Temple and Hatshepsut's Temple. There are temples to him at Elephantine Island and at Esna.

Khonsu – is the son of the god Amun and his wife Mut. He is the god of youth and the moon and was depicted either with the head of a falcon or as a mummiform child with a side-lock of hair. He wears a lunar disc sitting in a lunar crescent on his head. There is a temple dedicated to him in the Karnak complex.

Khonsu Temple – is in the near right-hand corner of the Karnak complex and is at present undergoing restoration. It was a very interesting temple with an 'Indiana Jones' feel about it and this aspect might now be lost. It is basically a New Kingdom Temple constructed by Ramses III on the site of an earlier temple. Many of its stone blocks have been taken from other temples on the site. There is an excellent view of Karnak from its roof which can be accessed through a narrow staircase and a small tip to the guard.

Kingfishers – although the familiar small blue European common kingfisher can be seen in Egypt, the bird you will see in great numbers in Luxor is the pied kingfisher which has striking black and white plumage and a beak that appears oversized for its body. They can be seen resting on posts all along the river bank; before they dash about over the river, hover for a few seconds and then plunge into the water to catch fish. They are territorial but only over a small area.

Kirat – is a land measure of 175 square meters. 24 kirats make up a feddan.

Kites – are a birdwatchers' delight and flocks of black kites can be seen performing aerial acrobatics and circling above the fields of the west bank early in the morning. They are graceful as they whirl and dive and then wheel off to their own hunting grounds. Another common sight, often seen sitting on the telegraph wires, is the striking black winged kite which is about the size of a kestrel and has largely grey and white plumage with black wings.

Klefti – is a slang term generally applied to a 'thief'. Arabic words have crept into the slang of the English language and conversely English originated words could have crept into Arabic. Klefti is possibly a derivative of 'Klefti Wallah' which was an Indian Raj term for thief and could have been introduced by British soldiers serving or training in Egypt at various times or by travellers stopping off in Egypt on their way home from India.

Kom Ombo – lies to the south of Luxor and is often visited on the way to Aswan. The temple there is Ptolemaic and was constructed over a period of one hundred years. It serves two gods. One half serves Sobek the crocodile god and the other half serves Horus the Elder. There are Roman additions and references to Apollo.

Koran – (Qur'an) is the sacred book of Muslims which was delivered to Mohammed (pbuh) and is considered as the direct word of Allah. The Koran (The Message) was delivered over a period of 23 years and consists of 114 chapters (surahs) of unequal length. The first surah of the Koran, the 'al fatiha', is used extensively in prayer.

Korsi – means 'chair' or 'seat' and is a word you will hear regularly when booking tickets on trains and buses or in the souk when a trader wishes you to sit down and share a cup of chai (tea) with him in the hope that you will buy something from his shop. Wheelchairs are also referred to as 'korsi'.

Kosoumak – is one of the worst forms of swear words but is often heard in heated arguments between Egyptian men. Its literal translation is 'your mother's genitals' - which has a four letter Anglo-Saxon equivalent in English.

Kromb – is cabbage and the cabbages in Upper Egypt grow to a tremendous size. Cabbage is not cooked in the same way as it is in Europe but is used in a similar way as vine leaves to wrap around savoury rice which is then steamed.

Kushari – is an inexpensive vegetarian dish greatly loved by Egyptians. It is made from, rice, macaroni, chick-peas and lentils topped with a tomato and onion sauce. There are several kushari restaurants in Luxor and the one in Station Street is highly recommended.

KV5 – each of the known tombs carries a reference to where it is and a number which indicates its position in the chronology of discovery. KV refers to the Valley of the Kings and the number five shows that it was the 5th tomb to be recorded. Although KV5 was found a long time ago its size and importance was not realised until the 1990s. Since then approximately 150 rooms have been found and it is believed to be the final resting place of many of Ramses II's sons. The tomb was badly sited and has suffered from intermittent flooding over the centuries and little of its decoration remains. It is filled with hardened flood-borne debris which will take Egyptologist Kent Weeks and his team many years to clear. The tomb is not open to the public and is unlikely to ever be opened as, apart from its sheer size, there is so little to see.

Luxor Temple

L
La – Lying

La – simply means 'no'. 'La Shokran' is 'no thank you'.

Lake Nasser – was formed after the construction of the Aswan High Dam which restricted the flow of the Nile. The lake is more than 500 km long. Thirteen temples, including Abu Simbel, Philae and Kalabsha, were saved from its rising waters but many important as yet undiscovered sites will have been lost. There are several cruise boats working on the Lake. Such a large body of water in what was dry desert has had a big impact on Luxor and Upper Egypt in that what should be an area of low humidity can become overwhelmingly stifling when evaporation from the lake gets trapped below cloud.

Land Disputes – land disputes are common in Luxor because on the death of a land owner the property can be split so many ways. Over the space of a couple of generations a large piece of land can have up to a hundred different owners. Tracing them all can be difficult and it only needs one to be omitted for the ownership of the land to be put in question. Very careful checks need to be made on any land or property purchase. If anybody is missed out then they usually insist that they own the piece of land right in the middle of the plot and have been known to put up a tent and live there until bought off and the matter settled.

Land Measurements – land is measured in kirats and feddans.

Lantern Restaurant – the Lantern is an excellent restaurant run by an Anglo/Egyptian couple (Debbie and Nasser) and specialises in English food. It is in Sherif el Rhoda Street which is almost opposite the Sonesta Hotel. It has an alcohol license and is probably the most successful restaurant in Luxor.

Lateen sail – is a triangular sail mounted at an angle to the main mast. In modern times, a spar has been added to the bottom of the sail making it more manoeuvrable. The dahabyias and feluccas have lateen sails.

Laundries – there are laundries and ironing shops throughout Luxor. Generally the cost of washing is 50 piastras per item with a further 50 piastras for ironing. Many people do their own washing and take it to a shop for ironing. Ironing shops are almost invariably run by men.

Law Samaht – means 'please' and is polite if you are asking someone to do something.

Lawyers – a list of English speaking lawyers is obtainable through the British Embassy. Although they provide the list they cannot guarantee the honesty of the lawyer. Sadly many of Luxor's lawyers are known to be incredibly corrupt and often represent both sides of a case totally ignoring any conflict of interest and pressing the case of the person who pays them the most. It is not unusual for vital papers in a case to go missing hours before it is being heard in court. Finding a good lawyer is not easy but it is not impossible and it is best to choose one through the recommendation of a past client.

Lay – means 'why' 'Lay la' is 'why not'.

LE – is the notation for the Egyptian Pound. It stands for 'Livre Egyptienne' which is a hangover from the days when there was considerable French influence in Egypt. The correct banking term for the Egyptian pound is EGP. The Arabic term for pound is 'ginnay' – 'ashera ginnay' is ten pounds.

Leb – are roasted water melon seeds and are offered for sale in paper cones by street vendors. Egyptians love them. You have to crack open the shell of the seed with your teeth and then eat the soft kernel that is inside.

Lemons – are of the small variety and are cheap and plentiful in Luxor. They are served with just about everything in Egyptian style restaurants. You may see young children selling them; sitting for many hours close to the ferry points. Fresh lemon juice is very refreshing.

Libraries – there are specialist libraries in the Chicago House and in the Heritage Centre but for most reading requirements the book collections in the hotels are adequate. You may have to ask at the reception desk about borrowing books but several of the hotels will lend books to non-residents. The Sheraton Hotel usually has a large collection of novels left by guests.

Little Britain – is actually Sherif el Rhoda Street and runs between Khaled Ibn el Walid Street and Medina Street. It is called Little Britain because of the large number of English style restaurants and businesses there.

Little Stars – is a successful charity with a focus on women and children that has been operating on the west bank in Qurna since 2007. It runs three free clinics for sick and disabled children, a free nursery school and a free training centre for women in addition to caring for 60 sponsored families who have around 350 children between them. It concentrates on health, education and relief of poverty.

Lizards – whenever you are outside in and around Luxor, if you look closely, you will see lizards running about. Mostly, they are small and move quickly. Some are brown and others striped. They are cold blooded and need the warmth of the sun to keep them active. There are also Monitor lizards which are large but they are rarely seen and keep to the canals. The lizards that hide behind the pictures in rooms are called geckos.

Locusts – were one of the plagues of Egypt and still plague it. In the spring of 2013 swarms of locusts were logged heading for Luxor but they then veered off towards Hurghada, eventually ending up over Cairo. If not checked they can cause immense harm and clear crops in minutes.

Lower Egypt – is the northern area of Egypt and is so called because it is in the lower reaches of the Nile. Upper and Lower Egypt were separate countries until unified by King Narmer in 3000 BCE. The crown of Lower Egypt was red.

Lust – Egyptian men can be lusty and some, having seen too many soft-porn films on the Internet and Satellite TV, may believe that western women can be promiscuous and that their lustful attentions will be welcomed rather than rebuffed. In Luxor, blatant offers of sex are frequent, upsetting and insulting but the men do not always realise this and think that they are complimenting you. The licentious actions of some holiday makers have made the situation worse and dressing in skimpy clothing advertises that you might be 'available'. This may not be fair, but it is a fact of life in non-European countries.

Luxor – has had various names. The ancient Egyptians called it Waset and the Greeks called it Thebes. Today it is known as Luxor which is a corruption of the Arabic 'al-uqsur' meaning 'the palaces'. Luxor lies at the bend of the river in Upper Egypt, is a tourist destination attracting thousands of visitors each year and will one day be the largest open air museum in the world.

Luxor Hotel – is one of the oldest hotels in Luxor, built by Thomas Cook's son John, as a base in Luxor for his cruise passengers, and at one time it rivalled the Winter Palace in opulence. In recent times it was owned by the Egyptian government and fell into disrepair. It has now been bought by an overseas investor and is being extensively enlarged and modernised to luxury standard.

Luxor Museum – is an excellent example of how museums should be laid out. The exhibits are interesting, relevant and well displayed. It is situated on the Corniche between Luxor and Karnak. Admission is 80 LE. It also holds the mummies of two Pharaohs – Ahmose, the first Pharaoh of the 18th dynasty, who liberated the country from the Hyksos, and Ramses I, the grandfather of Ramses II. On display is some magnificent statuary, which was found in a buried cache in Luxor Temple in 1989, and a reconstructed wall of stone bricks (talatat) featuring Pharaoh Akhenaten and his wife Nefertiti as well as the jewellery of Queen Ahhotep.

Luxor Temple – is dedicated to Amun and was built mainly by Amenhotep III and Ramses II but was added to by many more

Pharaohs, including Alexander the Great. It has a magnificent colonnade and has Greek and Roman additions at the rear. In Roman times, it served as the seat of government for Upper Egypt, and its grounds were converted into a Legionary headquarters. The greatly revered mosque to Abu el Haggag is within the temple precinct. The main purpose of the temple appears to be to serve as a focus for the annual Opet fertility festival, processional scenes from which adorn the walls of the colonnade. It is floodlit at night and open until 9.00 pm. Admission fee is 50 LE.

Luxor Times – is a monthly English-language magazine owned by Mena which reports news, social activities and archaeological developments in the town.

Lying – is endemic in tourist areas throughout the world when traders try to convince you of the authenticity of their wares but it is said that 'Egyptian men never lie; they simply invent their own truth'. Once it is said it becomes 'fact'. This is done mainly to defuse any situation but it arises from a complete refusal to accept responsibility for anything and everything that might be blamed on them no matter how guilty they are. Gigolos are expert liars; they have to be believed for them to be successful.

A Bedroom at El Moudira Hotel

M

Ma'as Salaam - Mut Precinct

Ma'as salaam – is a formal goodbye. It means 'peace go with you'.

Maat – is the goddess that represents truth and order, saving the world from chaos. She wears the feather of truth on her head against which souls (hearts) are weighed before they can enter the Afterlife. Although Deir el Medina is known as 'set Maat' meaning 'the place of truth' the temple there is dedicated to Hathor. There are no temples specifically dedicated to Maat.

Mabrouk – means 'congratulations'. 'Alf mabrouk' means 'one thousand congratulations.'

Mafeesh – means 'all gone, finished'. 'Mafeesh felous', ('money finished') is an answer to being harassed for baksheesh.

Magnoon – means 'crazy'. 'Inta magnoon' means 'you are crazy.'

Mahatta – is Arabic for 'station'. Sharia Mahatta is Station Street.

Malesh – the word 'malesh' is meant to comfort and console but it usually just infuriates. It means 'everything is OK', 'nothing has happened', 'it is not important', or 'forgive and forget', when in fact something you consider to be very important or quite awful could have happened that you are not in the least bit ready to forgive and forget about. It is a word that you will hear frequently in Luxor. It is not meant to dismiss an incident but is meant to try and make you feel better. I suppose it is a bit like saying 'You still have your hand so it's not that important' when you have sliced open a thumb and are bleeding everywhere.

Malqatta – means the 'place where things are picked up' and it is well named as there are shards of pottery everywhere. It is the site of the mud brick pleasure palace of Amenhotep III and covers a vast area to the south of the Medinet Habu on the west bank. The palace was abandoned by Amenhotep's son Akhenaten when he moved his family to Tel el Armana and is probably where his son Tutankhamun spent his childhood but it could have been re-inhabited by Tutankhamun when he became Pharaoh and may have been in use beyond the Ptolemaic period.

Marhaba Souk – the Marhaba souk is a new shopping area that was created to replace one at the side of the Winter Palace Hotel that was demolished during the renovation of the town. It is situated at the back of the Luxor Hotel. Many of the shops are still empty as the site was still incomplete at the start of the revolution but will soon fill up when the tourist situation improves as every shop has a tenant.

Markets - there is a local market every day in Luxor's Egyptian souk off El Hussein Street on the east bank of the river but the main market day is Tuesday with smaller markets being held on Saturdays. On the west bank there is a huge open market in the village of El Genena close to Qurna Hospital every Tuesday starting at about 6.00 am and ending at lunch time. There is a smaller market in the same place on Saturdays. These are not tourists markets selling souvenirs, they are produce markets with some livestock and are an excellent way of observing local life.

Marriage – in Islam a man is allowed 4 wives at any one time but a woman is allowed only one husband. However, very few Muslim men ever take more than one wife. Copts are allowed only one wife and divorce is not possible. The weddings that you see in the town have little to do with marriage ceremonies. The couple could have been married for some time before this celebration takes place. The 'wedding' merely announces that they are ready to live together and consummate the marriage. Village girls often enter marriage at a much younger age than the more educated girls in town. In the villages marriage at 14 years old is not uncommon although the legal minimum age for marriage in Egypt is currently 18 for both males and females. Certain elements of the Legislative Assembly are pressing for the legal minimum to be reduced (for girls) to 14 or even younger.

Massage – several of the bigger hotels employ masseurs and you will often find them on the cruise boats too. There are a couple of freelance European masseurs in Luxor who will come to your home. Men can usually get a massage at one of the gymnasiums such as the Star Gym off Medina Street.

McDonald's – the burgers in McDonald's have been adapted to the Egyptian taste and although liberally covered in mayonnaise are still palatable. It is situated in Luxor Temple Street, is air conditioned and has a free Wi-Fi Internet connection. Offers home deliveries.

Measurements – Egypt has a decimal measurement system of litres and millilitres for liquids, kilograms and grams for weights and metres and centimetres for linear sizing. However, it still retains the old land measurements of kirats and feddans for agriculture and building.

Medamud – has one of the 4 Montu temples around Luxor. It is situated about 10 km from Karnak and is not open to the public. Most of the remains are Ptolemaic in origin and at one time it was linked to Karnak by a canal - the remains of the original quayside are still there.

Medicines – most medicines can be bought over the counter in Luxor without a prescription. There are pharmacies in almost every street. If you need an injection, the pharmacist will carry out the procedure at the back of his shop. The prices of all medicines are written in Arabic on the packet but some pharmacies are known to grossly overcharge tourists. Also there is, unfortunately, a high preponderance of fake medicines in Egypt.

Medina Street – runs between Television Street and the Movenpick Road. At the Television Street end it is a narrow shopping street with a variety of shops and market stalls but at the other end it becomes a dual carriageway and is where Luxor Police Station, Fire Station and the prison are all located.

Medinet Habu - is the mortuary temple of Ramses III and its name means 'City of Habu' although it is unclear exactly who or what Habu was. The temple was dedicated to Amun as well as to Ramses himself. The outer wall is a magnificent example of its genre and the gatehouse where you enter the temple grounds is unique. The inner walls have some excellent reliefs showing the battle of the 'sea peoples' with some interesting instructions on keeping count of smitten enemies. In the shaded areas there is a lot of colour left in the murals that adorn the walls and ceilings. This temple was converted into a Coptic cathedral and even had its own bishop up until around 1,400 AD. Although a great deal of destruction occurred during the Christian occupation, it remains one of Egypt's best preserved and comprehensively documented temples. The temple also holds the chapel of the tombs of the Adoratrix as well as some earlier chapels. To the south of the temple lie the foundations of one of Ramses III's palaces and, to the north, the remains of a sacred lake. This is an exquisite temple and is often quiet as it is not on the main itinerary of the big tour groups. Admission is 30 LE.

Merenptah – even though he was the thirteenth and not the eldest son, by virtue of outliving his elder brothers, Merenptah jumped the succession queue and became Pharaoh when his father Ramses II died. His mortuary temple is close to the west bank ticket office and can be visited but it is of more interest to Egyptologists than to sightseers. The temple was largely constructed of bricks taken from the nearby mortuary temple of Amenhotep III and contained a stela referring to conquests, in what is now modern day Palestine, which states 'Israel is laid waste. Her seed is no more.' This is the only mention of Israel in any ancient Egyptian site. His tomb in the Valley of the Kings (KV8) is of far greater interest as it is one of the largest and has recently been cleaned and restored. His enormous granite outer sarcophagus has been painstakingly reconstructed from fragments found in the tomb and elsewhere.

Meretseger – 'she who loves silence' lives on the mountain and is a goddess of particular importance to the people who built the necropolis as she was believed to protect them from scorpions and snakes but she had venom which would blind dishonest workers. Only truly repentant workers could appeal to her for mercy and have their sight restored. She is shown as a coiled cobra or as a snake with a woman's head. She has a rock cut shrine on the track between the Valley of the Queens and Deir el Medina.

Metropolitan Café – is a pleasant outdoor café on the lower level of the Corniche close to the Winter Palace. However, it can be overwhelmed with diesel fumes if there are too many cruise boats moored close by. It no longer serves alcoholic drinks.

Meya meya – indicates one hundred per cent and is often used when asking someone how they are. It says that all is well.

Min – is a very ancient Egyptian fertility god dating to pre-dynastic times but by the New Kingdom era he was linked with Amun. His image is seen extensively and he is usually shown with black skin, an erect penis and a flail in his right hand. He has feathers on his headdress. Stories about Min have been manufactured for the tourist trade and images of him with an elaborately enlarged penis can be found in most of the tourist bazaars.

Min Fadlak – means 'excuse me' and is used if you are trying to attract a waiter or wish someone to move.

Minaret – is a tall structure attached to a mosque. Apart from being an indication of where a mosque is, it is used as a vantage point from which to call people to prayer. The call to prayer is made by the muezzin. Problems arose in one of the local villages south of Luxor when a church tower was raised, making it stand higher than a village minaret.

Mineral Water – is available just about everywhere and costs around 2 LE per litre upwards depending on where you buy and whether there is a shortage. Hotel prices for water are significantly higher than in the local shops. Imported mineral waters are very expensive. For health reasons, it is recommended that tourists drink bottled water and please make sure that the seal has not been broken. This is not because the water in Luxor is unfit for drinking but because it is so heavily chlorinated that if you are not used to it, it can upset your stomach.

Minya – lies to the north of Luxor about halfway between Luxor and Cairo. It is an agricultural area with a large Christian population and several active monasteries. Every now and then tribal disputes arise between local bango-growing drug barons which disrupts travel as Europeans are then barred from using the trains between Luxor and Cairo.

Mish - means 'not'; – 'Mish momkin' means 'not possible'; 'mish fahim' means 'not understand'; 'mish arif' means 'I don't know' .

MMD Club – (or MAD Club) is not an actual place but is a simple reference to those who are in denial after falling for the patter of a gigolo. It is an acronym of 'My Mohammed (or Ahmed) is Different'. Members have a tendency to convince themselves that their husband/lover actually is different from all the other gigolos and is really a faithful and honest partner even after he has been proven to be otherwise.

Moalla – is a village about 30km south of Luxor. It has several tombs dating from the 9th Dynasty which is the earliest in the area. Two are open to the public but tickets must be obtained from Luxor Temple, prior to journeying there.

Mobile Phones – no matter how poor a family is they are likely to own a mobile phone. Even if it is a very aged one and there is no credit on it, it will still be lovingly possessed. Egyptian men seem to be surgically attached to them and you will rarely see a man without one clamped to his ear, including while he is driving or riding a donkey. It can be particularly terrifying when your taxi driver is staring at the mobile's screen to read a text while negotiating traffic at speed. When travelling by train you will hear mobile phones ringing constantly night and day as families check every five minutes on the progress of various travellers. Mobile phones have given girls a freedom to talk to boys that their mothers never could have imagined. The local mobile phone companies are Mobinil, Vodafone and Etisalat.

Mobile Phone Shops – there are even more mobile phone shops in Luxor than there are clothes shops. Egyptians are as obsessed with mobile phones as Europeans were a decade ago and the shops seem to all remain in business but must have now reached saturation point. They all sell top-up services and cards as well as phones and most can recharge satellite dongles.

Mohammed (pbuh) – there are twenty-six prophets named in the Koran the majority having biblical connections; Adam being the first. Mohammed is considered as the final messenger of Islam rather than its founder. He was born in Mecca around 570 CE and spent his adult life spreading the word of the one god. He died in 632 CE and is buried in Medina. Islam is now a world religion with billions of followers.

Mollahyia – is a greatly favoured thick green gooey vegetable dish that is served with most Egyptian meals. Like Marmite and Vegemite, (yeast extract) you either love it or hate it.

Montu – is the falcon-headed god of war. He wears two feathers and a sun disc on his head and can carry various weapons. His temples were at Medamud, Armant, El Tod and the Precinct of Montu in the Karnak complex.

Montu Precinct – is situated within Karnak temple, adjacent to the Ptah temple. It is not open to the public and will take many years to restore. (Medamud, Armant and Montu can be visited though for a small amount of baksheesh!)

Moses – is an old-testament prophet who is credited with parting the Red Sea and leading the slaves out of Egypt and into the Promised Land. There is no record of Moses in Egyptian history and if he existed it could have been in the time of several different Pharaohs. Was he a Prince of Egypt brought up by a Princess after being found in the Nile's bulrushes or was he simply a protesting builder? There are several contenders for the role of being the Pharaoh who upset Moses: Ramses II at Pi Ramses; Akhenaten at Tel el Armana; and Merenptah in Luxor. The absence of Merenptah's mummy gave credence to the story as he was then considered to have been lost when the Red Sea closed over his army but his mummy was unsurprisingly discovered in 1898 (in the cache in KV35) and now lies in Cairo Museum.

Mosques – ('mastij') the oldest mosque in Luxor is in Luxor Temple and the most opulent is the new mosque in Medina Street. None of the mosques have the beauty, size and style of the mosques seen in Cairo but they are all well cared for and well attended. When entering a mosque, as a mark of respect, shoes must be removed and women must cover their hair.

Mosquitoes – ('namoose') Luxor's mosquitoes can be voracious at all times but are even more active at sunset. Some people have a very bad reaction to the bites and should use a repellent at all times, particularly if they are going on the river or are sitting close by it. Mosquitoes appear to find the lower legs, feet and ankles the most attractive. Fortunately Luxor is not in a malaria belt. OFF is a very effective deterrent and can be bought in most pharmacies. Anthisan is a good remedy to stop any bites itching.

Motor Bikes – ('makina') there has been a proliferation of cheap Chinese motor bikes in Luxor and you will see them being used as transport for the whole family – including babies. The death rate among young male riders is high. Motor bikes can be hired for day use but it is not recommended as roads are lethally potholed. Crash helmets are a legal requirement but are seldom worn. Builders' plastic hard hats are often used as a substitute and they are usually worn unfastened making them even more useless. It is very alarming to see a man wearing an unfastened builder's hat riding a motor cycle with two small children squashed between him and his wife who is sitting side-saddle behind him carrying a small baby.

Motor Boats – motor boats are used to carry passengers from one side of the river to the other. If you wish to commandeer one for your personal use the average price is 5 LE for the direct route from one ferry point to another. If you wish to use the boats to go elsewhere then negotiate a price before the journey starts. If you cross the river in a shared boat then expect to pay 1 LE. It is not wise for lone women to commandeer a motor boat after dark unless she knows the driver as it could send out the wrong message about her sexual availability.

Moudira Hotel – is a luxurious 5* hotel on the west bank (not close to the river) with a successful faded chic style. It was designed and managed by a woman, who scoured the antique markets of Lebanon and Cairo for items to decorate the hotel. It took her name as 'Moudira' is the Arabic female form for 'manager'.

Moulid – means Birthday and is usually used to celebrate individual saints but it is a traditional rather than a religious event and is frowned upon by clerics. The main Moulids in the Luxor area are Abu el Haggag which is held annually three weeks before the start of Ramadan and the Coptic 'Mari Girgis' which takes place in Armant. There are several other memorial moulids held on the west bank which involve fairs and displays of horsemanship.

Movenpick Road – the Movenpick Road was renamed the Mubarak Highway before the Revolution in 2011 but the name did not stick and it quickly reverted to its old name The road takes its name from the Movenpick Hotel which is on its route. The hotel is now known as the Jolie Ville but the road still carries the old name.

MSA – is the Ministry of State for Antiquities which is the reformed Supreme Council for Antiquities that has responsibility for all the temple and tombs in Egypt. Excavations cannot be done without their permission.

Mud Bricks – have been used for building for thousands of years and are still used extensively in the villages in Upper Egypt. Mud is mixed with straw or sugar cane waste, shaped and then left to dry in the sun. Unfortunately mud cracks when it is too dry and dissolves when it is too wet so it is not an ideal building material but, as the bricks can be made by a family at little or no cost, it is a way of obtaining a home when none other is available.

Muezzin – is the person who is appointed to call the faithful to prayer. Originally he would have to make his voice heard but now the minarets are fitted with loudspeakers.

Muftah – muftah is Arabic for 'key' and is a word that might come in handy if you are staying in a local hotel.

Muftah Inglesi – is an 'English Key' which is actually a spanner. Most households have a huge spanner which is used for attaching valves to the gas cylinders needed for cooking.

Mufti – to the British 'mufti' is the wearing of civilian clothes by military personnel but it is also an Islamic scholar who is able to interpret the Koran. The highest official of Islamic law is the Grand Mufti. In Egypt this office is held by Shawki Ibrahim Abdel-Karim.

Mummification – it took 70 days to complete the mummification process of a dead body. First the body was washed then an incision made into the left side to remove the lungs, liver, stomach and intestines. These were dried and then either put back inside the body or stored in canopic jars. The heart was left in place as the centre of intelligence. Next the brain was hooked and removed through the nose. The body was then packed in natron so that it dried out. When there were no fluids left in the body it was oiled, the body cavity packed with linen or straw, to preserve its appearance in life, and then wrapped in strips of linen. Amulets were placed between the layers to protect the body and a scroll from the Book of the Dead, carrying instructions on how to enter the Afterlife, was placed in the mummy's hands. (See Royal Mummies.)

Mummification Museum – is part of a complex on the riverbank side of the Corniche. The museum is worth a visit as it is well presented and clearly shows the mummification process. There is a lecture theatre in the complex where weekly Egyptology Lectures are given in the winter months by visiting archaeologists who are working on the local temples and tombs.

Murders – considering the more than occasional volatility of the Egyptian temperament there are surprisingly few murders in Luxor and those that do occur are usually domestically driven or arise from family feuds. There was a proven case of murder more than a decade ago which involved a female British tourist but she was actually poisoned by her British husband and apart from that no murders have involved tourists. 2013 started with 4 Egyptian murders within the space of a few days followed by another 4 later in the year. This is far fewer than would be found in most towns of a comparable size and actually demonstrates how peaceful the town is. In one case 2 men died following an accusation of paedophilia and in another case two elderly women were killed in their home for unknown reasons. Later, three women in one family died in honour killings and a young man was mutilated possibly also in an honour killing. Throughout the whole of the two troubled years of revolution only one Luxor tourist was killed and that was in the crossfire of a tribal dispute. However, it cannot be ignored that in 1997 there was a major incident which led to the loss of 64 lives at Hatshepsut's Temple.

Museums – there are two museums in Luxor both of which are on the Corniche; the Mummification Museum and Luxor Museum. However, Luxor is set to be the largest open-air museum in the world. The papyrus museums referred to by calleche drivers are actually shops.

Music – Egyptians love music and, wherever you stay in Luxor, at some time or other you are likely to hear music blaring from loudspeakers. Loud music is played into the small hours of the morning at shop openings, weddings and all celebrations.

Muslim – is the name given to followers of Islam and the prophet Mohammed (pbuh). 90% of Luxor's population are Sunni Muslims which means that they are basically orthodox and accept that Abu Bakr was his rightful successor. 85% of the world's Muslims are Sunni.

Mut – in the ancient Egyptian language Mut meant mother. Mut was an important goddess as the wife of Amun and the mother of Khonsu. She is shown with the crowns of Upper and Lower

Egypt on her head and the feather of Maat at her feet. She is sometimes shown with the wings of a white vulture and has been worshiped from early dynastic times. Her main temple, which was rebuilt by Hatshepsut, is in the Karnak precincts.

Mut Precinct - is part of the Karnak complex, not yet open to the public. Excavations there are still on-going, and much 18th dynasty construction is being found.

Nefertari

N
Nagar Market – Nus

Nagar Market – is situated on the main road close to Qurna hospital and is the largest supermarket on the west bank. Deliveries can be arranged.

Nakhil Hotel – is a pleasant hotel and restaurant set in the Gezera Village part of the west bank and not on the Ramla.

Names – in Egypt, the history of a family is shown by a person's name. The first name is the given name, the second name is the father's name, the third is the family name and the fourth is the grandfather's name. So, it is quite possible for someone to be called Mohammed Mohammed Mohammed Mohammed. Women's names follow the same pattern with their given name being followed by the father's name etc. Women do not change their name when they marry but retain their father's name throughout their life. In ancient Egyptian religions, names contained power and through learning his real name, Isis tricked Ra into giving her the power to restore Osiris. In ancient Egypt it was believed that if your name was written down somewhere then your existence in this life and the Afterlife was assured. The god Thoth wrote the name of each king, in confirmation of his right to rule, on the leaves of the sacred persea tree and there are beautiful reliefs of this scene on the north and south walls of the hypostyle hall at Karnak Temple and in the Ramesseum. (See Cartouche).

National Bank of Egypt – has a branch on the Corniche and in the Winter Palace Hotel. It has an after-hours currency exchange service that is open until 9.00 p.m. in summer.

National Holidays - Egypt appears to have an abundance of religious and secular festivals and national holidays which is entertaining but can cripple business as everything shuts down for the duration. The main Muslim festivals are Ramadan, Eid el Fitr, Eid al Adha and the Birthday of Mohammed. Coptic holidays include Christmas, Easter, New Year and the Feast of St. George. Secular holidays include Labour Day, Liberation Day (October 6th), Armed Forces Day and many others. A new Revolution Day holiday has been added to the list, commemorating the 25th January uprising against Mubarak.

National Service – except for medical reasons, where there is more than one son in a family, males are expected to complete national service in the army. The length of service can be from one year to three years depending on the level of education the conscript has. National Service used to be barred for men with foreign wives and was used as an excuse for marrying older women outside their culture. With a foreign wife and the correct bribes, national service could be avoided; but this is no longer the case. However, it is still used as a way to con women out of money.

Natron – is a naturally occurring salt mixture that was harvested directly from dry lake beds in Egypt and was used extensively in the mummification process as it absorbs moisture and creates a hostile environment for bacteria. When blended with castor oil it makes a smokeless fuel which was used by the artisans to light the tombs they were working on without staining them with soot. It was also used in making ceramics and glass.

Necropolis – the necropolis of ancient Waset/Thebes stretches the length of the Theban hills and is a UNESCO World Heritage site. The necropolis consists of the tombs of Pharaohs, Queens, Princes and consorts set in the Valley of the Kings, the Western Valley and the Valley of the Queens. There are also many notable tombs of artisans and noblemen and their families dotted around the necropolis. They are in an area apart from the Royal tombs but close enough to gain vicarious kudos through their proximity to the living gods. There are also numerous mortuary temples of New Kingdom Pharaohs in various states of preservation. Temples specifically dedicated to gods are to be found close to, but not part of, the main necropolis.

Nefertari – was the beloved wife of Ramses II (Ramses the Great) and bore him several sons but they appear to have all predeceased him. There are statues of their daughters in the temple that Ramses dedicated to her at Abu Simbel. Popular fiction portrays Ramses as a monogamous devoted husband who was faithful to his wife and had adopted his sons but research indicates otherwise and shows that he may have had over two hundred children, some of them by his own daughters. Nefertari's tomb is spectacular but its decoration suffered badly from its popularity among tourists. The tomb was closed for restoration in the 1990s at a cost of $6m dollars. It took five years to complete but when the tomb was reopened it quickly became evident that even with severely restricted visitor numbers the tomb was still rapidly deteriorating and it was closed again, probably permanently.

Nefertiti – was the favourite wife of Amenhotep IV who later changed his name to Akhenaten and started the monotheistic cult of Aten the sun disc. Nefertiti shared his beliefs and played a large part in the creation of the new (later deserted) capital at Tel el Armana. Some Egyptologists think that she outlived her husband and carried on as Pharaoh for a few months after his death under other names before Tutankhamun ascended to the throne. (She was probably not his mother). Her image is well known through the beautifully painted limestone bust that was found in an uncovered workshop in Tel el Armana and is now shown in the Neues Museum in Berlin. Egypt is constantly asking for the return of this precious item from its past.

Nephthys – is sister of Osiris and Isis and wife of her brother Seth. She is the mother of Anubis who was fathered by her brother Osiris. She stands guard over the bodies of the deceased in the form of a winged kite and is shown with a hieroglyph on her head which resembles a bowl on a stand and represents her name, 'Lady of the Mansion'.

Newspapers – there are several newspapers in English format that would be of interest to tourists, Al Ahram being easiest to obtain. Al Ahram and The Egyptian Independent also have online versions and there is an online version of Al Ahram's weekly edition. Other online sources of news are the BBC World, CNN, and Al Jezeera. Luxor Portal requires a translating package. There is a locally produced English-language monthly magazine called Luxor Times.

Nightlife – Luxor does not have a wealth of nightlife but an increasing number of hotels (such as the Nile Palace Hotel) are now offering in-house evening entertainment. This is likely to increase as the major tourist companies move towards all-inclusive holidays and wish to keep their guests on site. There used to be several discos operating but they were mainly just pick-up joints frequented by gigolos and lonely travellers and they closed when tourist numbers plummeted.

Nile Monitor Lizard – is also known as a River Leguaan but is locally referred to as a Warren. It can grow up to 3 metres long and is muscular with powerful legs and strong jaws so it is often mistaken for a crocodile. They live mainly in the canals and feed on fish, carrion and small mammals when they can catch them.

Nile Palace Hotel – is 5* and situated in Khaled Ibn el Walid Street and used to be called Le Meridien. It is now owned by the Steigenberger group and has evening entertainment, including a demonstration of Sufi Dancing, in an attractive open internal atrium.

Nile, River – is comprised of the Blue and the White Niles and is 6650 km (4,130 miles) long. It is the longest river in the world and at Luxor it is approximately 500 metres wide. Its most distant source is still undetermined but may be in Rwanda so it is measured from Lake Victoria. It is Egypt's lifeline as its waters are used to irrigate otherwise lifeless desert. In ancient times the annual inundation of the Nile, which led to the deposit of fertile black silt, helped make Egypt the breadbasket of the known world. The Nile's waters are now controlled by the Aswan dam and there is an on-going dispute with other Nile dependent countries over treaties which govern water extraction that appear to be overly favourable to Egypt. At present, (2013) there is tension between Egypt and Ethiopia over Ethiopia's proposed damming of the Blue Nile. There are several ways of crossing the river: the tourist ferry operates 24 hours a day, and costs 1 LE for tourists; motorboats operate on both sides of the river if you prefer a faster crossing; and Luxor Bridge, the only road crossing for 60 km, is about 12 km south of Luxor

Nile Valley Sunbirds – are seen in Luxor. During most of the year both sexes look the same and are unimposing but in February at the beginning of the mating season the male acquires fantastic glossy green plumage and a bright sulphur-yellow belly.

Nilometer – is a means of judging the clarity and depth of the river and enabled priests to predict the strength of the inundation on which Egypt depended. Being able to make these predictions was part of the mysteries of the priesthood. Nilometers are found in several temples including the Temple of Horus at Edfu and Seti I Temple on the west bank. There are also remains of one at Medinet Habu. They are accessed by steps and descend to the water table.

Niqab – is the veil that covers the face of Muslim women. Niqabs were rare in Luxor but are now more frequently seen.

Nobles' Tombs – several nobles' tombs are open to the public and all are worth visiting although some are more richly decorated than others. The walls of these tombs often have scenes depicting daily life and the activities of the tomb owner and have given us much information about the lives of the ordinary Egyptians. The most famous is perhaps the tomb of the vines which belonged to Prince Sennefer who was vintner to Amenhotep II. His tomb and the tombs of Rekhmire, Userhet, Roy and several others are open to the public. Tombs of lesser importance can be seen on the upper reaches of Theban Hills standing out like rows of large black teeth. There are also tombs of significant artisans in the Workers' Village (Deir el Medina).

Nubia – covered northern Sudan and southern Egypt and had a mainly troubled relationship with Egypt although several of the ancient Egyptian Pharaohs are thought to have had Nubian origins. Part of Nubia was annexed and incorporated into Egypt but Egypt was actually defeated and occupied by Nubia in the 25th dynasty. Luxor appears to have been regularly threatened by Nubians over its history. By facing towards Nubia, the temple at

Abu Simbel served two purposes; it served the gods as a place of worship and openly displayed the might of Egypt.

Numbers – Arabic numbers are easy for Europeans to follow as Europe adopted the Arabic numbering system when it abandoned Roman numerals which had made multiplication and division impossible. Only the ways in which some of the numbers are written differ. The numbers are written in the same order as European numbers but are read from right to left and semi-reversed when spoken. For instance 25 becomes five and twenty – 'khamsa ashreen'. 125 becomes 'meya khamsa ashreen'. (One hundred five and twenty). One – wahid: two – itnayn; three – talata; four – arbaa; five – khamsa; six – sitta; seven- saba; eight – tamanya; nine – tessa; ten - ashera.

Nus – means 'half'. When you ask someone if they speak English they may answer 'nus wa nus' (half and half) indicating that they are not fluent.

Om Hashim Restaurant

O

Oasis – Ostraca

Oasis – trips to the Oases of the western desert (Kharga, Ferafra and Dakhla) can be arranged from Luxor. Siwa is the most famous but is more easily reached from Cairo. It was the home of the Oracle of Amun who was visited by both Herodotus and Alexander the Great.

Obelisks – derive their name from the Greek word for 'pointed pillar' and are thought to portray a petrified sun ray. They were usually erected in pairs at the entrance of temples and, despite their enormous size, they appear to have been too attractive to ignore as souvenirs right back to Roman times. There were eventually more obelisks in Rome than in the whole of Egypt. An obelisk is a monolithic stone that was hewn out of bedrock in the granite quarries of Aswan and elsewhere. Remember how crude the tools were; only tools made of copper and stone were available so this was a colossal task. (There is an unfinished obelisk in Aswan that demonstrates the process). When hewn, they were then hauled to the river and floated up to Luxor to be engraved and erected at various temples. Several of Luxor's obelisks were removed in the late 19th century and these, along with others removed from Alexandria, are dotted around Europe. There are three standing obelisks remaining in Luxor. Two are at Karnak Temple - one erected by Tutmosis I and one erected by Hatshepsut which is 30 metres high and weighs over 300 tonnes. (There are also the remains of another lying on its side.) Another one stands at the front of Luxor Temple. There were two, as was the custom, but one was removed and sent to France. It now stands in the Place de la Concorde. The obelisk that stands on the Embankment in London (Cleopatra's Needle) was originally erected in the Egyptian city of Heliopolis by Thutmose III, around 1450 BC, and not in Luxor.

Ogdoad – the Ogdoad, which was a group of eight Gods and Goddesses (Naunet and Nu, Amaunet and Amun, Kauket and Kuk, Hauhet and Huh) are credited with creation of the universe. There are variants of the myth originating in different parts of

Egypt but one myth recounts the laying of an egg on a mound at Medinet Habu from which sprang the bird of light and Ra the creator of the world.

Okra - ('bamia') has been cultivated in Egypt since ancient times and is commonly offered as a side dish with Egyptian meals. It is usually cooked with tomatoes and onions or else liquidised as a sauce and poured over rice.

Om – means 'mother' and many Egyptian curses involve insults to the virtue of an adversary's mother.

Om Ali – is a favourite Egyptian dessert. It is basically bread and butter pudding Egyptian style but made with cooked puff pastry instead of bread. It contains lots of cream plus coconut and almonds.

Om Hashim Restaurant – is at the El Hussein Street end of the Egyptian souk and is also known as Smokey Joe's due to the smoke from the open-sided kitchens. It offers excellent freshly cooked Egyptian food at reasonable prices. There is a new branch close by.

Om Seti – there are a lot of obsessed reincarnations resident in Luxor but the most famous reincarnation was Dorothy Eady, an Englishwoman who lived in Abydos and believed that Pharaoh Seti I had been her lover. She had one son with her Egyptian husband and named him Seti hence her 'mother of Seti' name.

Omar Market – was Luxor's first supermarket and is in Medina Street. It carries a wide range of food and household items and has recently been refurbished.

Opet Festival – is an ancient fertility festival which was held in the second month of the Nile flood when Amun's statue was taken from Karnak Temple to Luxor Temple where he could spend a three-week honeymoon with his celestial wife Mut. Due to its fertility nature, the festival is thought to have triggered several weeks of debauchery. There are reliefs in several of the temples (Luxor Temple and Medinet Habu) that show the parade and the fattened bulls to be slaughtered to Amun. The festival is still remembered through the Abu el Haggag moulid.

Opet Temple – is in the near right hand corner of the Karnak Temple site next to the Khonsu Temple and behind what must be the biggest jigsaw puzzle in the world. It has recently been restored by a French archaeological group. It was built by Nectanebo 1, modified in the Ptolemaic era and even embellished by the Roman Emperor Augustus. This particular temple has several crypts the largest of which acts as a symbolic grave for Amun.

Oranges – Egypt grows superb oranges and tangerines ('burto'aan') that can be bought from the markets for around 2.5 LE per kilo and the juice bars offer delicious freshly pressed orange juice for a small sum.

Orfi – means common law and is usually applied to the temporary contract marriages that allow couples to cohabit. Orfi marriages are not officially recognised as legal marriages outside of Egypt but visiting women often enter such arrangements as marriage papers are required if a foreign women is to live or share a room with an Egyptian man. Egyptian couples who are not in a financial position to marry formally sometimes enter these arrangements but orfi marriages are frowned upon and give women no rights even if there are children. If the orfi papers are not registered with the court they can be torn up and discarded if the relationship finishes but if they have been registered with the court than formal proceedings have to be followed to end the relationship.

Organised Tours - many visitors take tours arranged by their original tour company but are unaware that there are several local tour companies such as Karnak Travel, Jolley's and Petra Travel that offer identical tours at a much lower cost per person. As with all things, shop around for the best deal, not just what your tour leader offers.

Orphan – many of the children considered as orphans are actually abandoned babies of unmarried mothers. There is no culture of acceptance of unmarried mothers and many would be subject to abuse and punishment for loss of family honour so the babies are abandoned in empty buildings etc. Children who are genuinely orphaned are usually cared for within the extended family. In Islam a child is only considered an orphan until reaching thirteen years old. There is no full adoption procedures in Islam and a child must retain its father's name (if known) but fostering of children is increasing.

Orphanages – there are several orphanages in Luxor run by Muslims and Copts but the most well-known is the Sunshine Home which is situated off the Movenpick Road.

Osirion – despite Luxor having a large necropolis, there are no temples to Osiris actually in Luxor. The nearest is in Abydos where there is an underground temple specifically dedicated to him. It is a very eerie place as it is below ground level and often partially flooded with green water. Just as Seti's temple at Abydos is the Temple of Osiris the Osirion could be thought of as the Tomb of Osiris.

Osiris – is god of the Underworld but is associated with renewal. He is brother/husband of Isis and father of Horus. He usually has green skin and his legs are bandaged in mummified form. He holds a crook and flail across his body and his headdress has a large feather on each side. His brother Seth is his eternal enemy in a fight between good and evil. Seth had him murdered and dismembered but his sister/wife Isis restored him. Osiris is also the father of Anubis who was born to his other sister Nephthys. Although he is master of the Underworld he is associated with regeneration mainly because he could give the gift of eternal life and because he himself beat death.

Ostraca – are pot shards that were used for note writing; a bit like modern day 'post-its'. The have been found in great numbers at Malqatta and in the reservoir pit at Deir el Medina. Writings on the Deir el Medina ostraca cover such a wide range of topics that they give a detailed insight into daily life. Some have drawings on them which could be outline instructions for tomb decorations and others have lists of names that could have been work schedules. Many show love letters, erotica and poetry.

A Restored Pyramid over a Tomb at Deir el Medina

P

P – Pyramids

P – there are several sounds in the Arabic language that do not appear in the English language but the opposite also applies as there is no P sound or symbol anywhere in Arabic.

Paedophilia – where there is poverty there is vulnerability and there are always those who will take advantage of it. Several European men have been refused re-entry to Luxor because of their association with children but others have escaped justice. Vigilante action, leading to deaths, has been used recently in Luxor against Egyptian men who have been accused of abusing children.

Painters – most of the delightful atmospheric prints you see of old Egypt were painted by David Roberts in the mid-19th century and you can buy copies in any of the bookshops. There are several galleries showing modern paintings - one in Khaled Ibn el Walid Street and others in St. Joseph's Street and Sherif el Rhoda Street.

Paper – you can buy writing paper or printer paper inexpensively at any stationery shop (there are several in Station Street) but high quality paper is hard to find. 70 gsm paper costs about 25 LE per ream. There is a large mill at Qus which turns sugar cane waste into paper and plans are in hand for a women's cooperative to make hand-made banana leaf paper for letter writing and card making.

Papyrus – is formed by pressing together strips of the papyrus reed and is the forerunner of paper. The strips are first laid one way, then covered with another layer at right angles and then pressed to produce a natural glue that binds the layers together. It can be rolled without cracking and is very long lasting as shown by the many ancient scrolls that are still in existence. Most of the papyrus paintings offered for sale are stamped rather than hand drawn but they still make attractive gifts. Beware of banana leaf imitations that crack when rolled. The papyrus reed is no longer widespread in Egypt and the vast marshes of reeds shown in the tomb paintings have long gone, but papyrus is grown commercially in the Fayoum area where papyrus preparation is a huge industry.

Papyrus 'Museums' – there are no papyrus museums in Luxor. The places that calleche drivers promise to take you to are really shops where they get commission on anything that you buy.

Parcels – when you return home you may feel that you would like to send presents to the friends that you made while in Luxor. All parcels are opened by the authorities and the contents assessed for suitability and value. The customs charges can be high. In one instance, a local man was advised of a parcel waiting for him at the post office. He was not advised of its contents. The duty to be paid was 200 le. He paid the fee and then discovered that the parcel contained two books that he could not read. As his monthly salary at that time was only 300 le, while meaning to help the man, the present had actually cost him and his family dearly. For sending parcels from Luxor, a Customs Officer will want to check the contents, so it is best to take the wrapping and contents to the post office and wrap it there under supervision.

Pasha – pronounced 'Basha' is an honorific title similar to calling someone 'Sir' and is widely used by Egyptian men when addressing their friends.

Passport – if you lose your passport you will need to apply to your embassy in Cairo for a replacement as there are no consulate services in Luxor. Do not risk losing your passport in a bag snatch so leave it safely in your hotel but carry a photocopy of it with you.

Passport Office – the passport office is in Khaled Ibn el Walid Street opposite the Nile Palace Hotel. If you need to extend your visa to stay in Egypt then this is where you apply. You will need a passport size photograph and photocopies of your passport details and present visa.

Patience – you will find that your patience can be stretched to the limit with the Egyptian lack of a sense of time and a sometimes absent work ethic but shouting and yelling does not improve the situation. So sit down, breathe deeply and just accept that there is nothing that you can do to hurry anything along.

Pavements – pavements are exceptionally high and often have badly laid tiles ready to twist your ankles. Most people choose to brave the traffic and walk in the road than repeatedly climb up and down them.

Pbuh – is often quoted when the name of the prophet Mohammed is mentioned. It is a respectful 'peace be upon him'.

Peanuts – are known as 'foul Sudani', ('Sudanese beans') and are offered for sale in paper cones by Luxor's street vendors. They are salty, taste good and cost only a few piastras.

Pepper – Egyptians love spicy foods and are fond of adding chilli peppers ('shatta') to salads as well as cooked dishes. It can be alarming to bite into a salad and burn your mouth. When ordering a salad you might like to make it clear that you do not want chilli peppers in it. 'Mafeesh shatta' should accomplish this. Ordinary pepper is called 'filfil', with black pepper being 'filfil aswid' and white pepper being 'filfil abyad'.

Perfume Bottles – delicate and elaborately decorated glass perfume bottles of varying sizes are easily found in Luxor. They are attractive and inexpensive and make excellent gifts.

Perfume Oils – Egypt was famous throughout the ancient world for its wonderful perfumes which for centuries were its main export. The best perfume oils were produced in the Delta area. Creating perfumes was a skill as the order in which ingredients were blended was of great importance as the last one to be added had the greatest effect on the fragrance. They were oil and not alcohol based. One of the favourites consisted of oil from bitter almonds and unripe olives scented with cardamom, sweet rush, sweet flag, honey, wine, myrrh, seed of balsamum, galbanum and turpentine resin. Perfume oils are a concentrate and are now commercially mixed and diluted with alcohol. There are fake copies of well-known fragrances throughout Luxor. You can usually spot them by the misspellings on the packaging which otherwise looks genuine.

Pets – Egyptians do not generally keep pets. They tolerate cats but consider dogs to be dirty and are often afraid to touch them. However, pet food for both dogs and cats is available in the larger supermarkets and at Arkwright's in St. Joseph Street.

Pharaoh – is the title used to describe the rulers of ancient Egypt. In fact the rulers had many names including a Horus name and a Nome name. The word originates from in the term "pr-aah" which means "great house" and basically describes a royal palace. They were the semi-divine rulers of everything and everybody and were the absolute rulers of the earliest and greatest civilisations in history. The title generally passed to the eldest son of the favourite wife but there were many exceptions and diversions from this over the centuries. Pharaoh was considered the earthly representation of the gods and was responsible for maintaining well-being and order ('maat') through the constant supply of offerings to a multitude of gods. Pharaohs were usually depicted as wearing a headdress like the one on Tutankhamun's funerary mask, an ornately pleated kilt and a false beard. Even Hatshepsut is depicted as wearing a beard at times but not Cleopatra. Cleopatra is sometimes considered to be the last Pharaoh but this is not actually the case as the title passed on to the Roman emperors. Luxor has many monuments built by the Pharaohs throughout their history but the main ones seen by visitors are of the New Kingdom era whose Pharaohs built their mortuary temples on the west bank and were buried in the Valley of the Kings. The Pharaoh's absolute power has not been totally lost over the millennia as many Luxor men still act like Pharaohs inside their own homes.

Pharmacies – there is an extraordinary number of pharmacies in Luxor which reflects the nation's latent hypochondria and tendency to self-medicate. Most of the drugs that require prescriptions in Britain can be bought over the counter but more dangerous medications require a doctor's note.

Photocopying – it is better to carry a photocopy of your passport around with you than to carry the real thing and risk losing it. However, there are times when you need a further copy of it for official purposes like applying for a visa extension. Most of the big hotels have a Business Centre and will make copies for you and there are several shops around the town that offer photocopying services. The one most widely used, because it is closest to the Passport Office, is a photographic shop on the left-hand side of the street opposite the Sonesta St. George. The charge is either 25 or 50 piastras a copy or 1 LE if they see you coming.

Photographs - if you take photographs of people then expect to pay a small amount of 'baksheesh' for the privilege. You can take photographs anywhere except military installations and inside museums and tombs. Many of the wonderful old photographs that you see for sale were taken by the Gaddis family at the turn of the $19^{th}/20^{th}$ century. If you want to print your photographs in Luxor (far cheaper than in Britain, and of an equal quality) there are several places which provide a quick service – Amoun Digital at the bottom of Television Street, and the Fuji Shop near Luxor Temple, both give excellent service.

Pickles – are served with most meals and are made up of roughly cut carrots, cucumber, turnip which is stained pink with beetroot juice, onion and chilli peppers in sugar and white vinegar. Sometimes there are olives too. They are very strong and may also contain lumps of pickled lemons. They are sold from big tubs in shops and transferred to plastic pots or polythene bags. They are also sold at the street stalls as an accompaniment for falafel sandwiches.

Pigeons – ('hamaam') are kept for eating and are considered both a delicacy and an aphrodisiac that gives heightened sexual potency. They are usually stuffed with spiced rice and most of the Egyptian restaurants offer them on their menu. They are not for the hungry man though as the pigeons are small and have very little meat on them. There are pigeon lofts on the roofs of most village houses; some are ancient and very ornate.

Pigs – Muslims do not eat pork products of any kind but you can get ham and bacon from the Christian shops. Pigs are not bred in Luxor and recently great hardship was caused in Cairo when all the pigs there were culled following a scare over swine flu.

Pizzas – pizzas are as popular in Luxor as anywhere else in the world and there are several pizza restaurants in the town mainly based in Television Street. There is also an excellent pizza house called Café Roma in St. Joseph's Street.

Police –there are many different kinds of police in Luxor and all of them are armed. There are Tourist Police, River Police, Antiquities Police, Security Police, Traffic Police and Secret Police and the normal criminal chasing police. In additional there are local Gellabyia wearing policemen who carry rifles over their shoulders. The main general Police Station is at the Movenpick Road end of Medina Street. Security Police are seen in black uniforms at tourist sites and are now known as Central Security. The notorious Secret Police (Amn ad Dowla) were based next door to Luxor Museum but have apparently been disbanded following the 2011 revolution. In emergencies telephone 122. (See Tourist Police).

Population – The total population in Egypt was recorded at 82.5 million people in 2011. This is a rise of nearly 200% in the space of 50 years. 2012 estimates consider the real figure to be in excess of 92 million. This huge population expansion is causing major problems for the new administration. In 2010 the population of Luxor was measured at just under 500,000 people. There is a large expat population (mainly women) with British, Dutch, Danish and French making up the majority but there are only very rough estimates of their number. Visitors swell the numbers during the high-season winter months but there has been a marked drop in visitor numbers since the revolution of 2011.

Pope – Egypt has its own Coptic Pope and although the position is traditionally associated with Alexandria the actual seat has been in Cairo since 1047. In 2012 Pope Tawadros II was elected as the 118th Pope.

Post Office – there is a large Post Office at the temple end of Station Street (Sharia Mahatta). There is also a large Post Office in Qurna Gedida, the new village on the West Bank, and there is a sorting office at Seul.

Postage – postage rates are low compared with Europe. There are no problems over sending letters and cards overseas but all parcels will be opened and the contents inspected so it is best to take the wrapping and contents to the post office and parcel it up there in front of the customs officer.

Prayer – prayer differs according to religion. In Luxor most Christians are devout and attend church on Sunday. For them prayer is not obligatory and is akin to an act of offering thanks to God and asking for aid from various revered saints but in Islam it is a mandatory act of ritual worship. With certain exceptions, prayer is obligatory for all Muslims once they have reached puberty. There are five set prayer times during the day starting at dawn and ending at nightfall. Calls to prayer can be heard echoing all over the city. There are two public calls, the first is to alert people to the approaching prayer time so that they can wash and prepare themselves and the second is as prayer begins. Women are expected to pray but they are not admitted to the main part of the mosque as they might be a distraction to men. They are instructed to pray at home or are hived off to side-rooms and outhouses. In one of the largest Cairo mosques women are expected to pray in a nearby garage among cars in various state of repair. The women do not appear to object to this apparent discrimination.

Presents – from Europe are always greatly appreciated if they are given in person. If you are invited to a family home for a meal you may wish to take a small gift with you. Cakes, biscuits and sweets would be greatly appreciated by the whole family. (See Gifts.)

Princes and Princesses – as the Pharaohs had numerous wives and substantial harems, they produced a prodigious number of offspring. The royal family tended to marry among themselves to keep the bloodline pure but the widening of the gene pool was probably assisted by the sheer number of relatives from which to choose a wife or husband. In statues, daughters are usually shown in the company of their parents but sons are rarely shown in this way. However, there are famous processions of sons (and daughters) shown on the walls of the Ramesseum (Ramses II) and Medinet Habu (Ramses III). Most of the royal sons ended up being buried in the Valley of the Queens but a few did make it into the Valley of the Kings. KV5 was constructed for the sons of Ramses II and KV19 for Prince Mentuherkhepshef who was a son of Ramses IX. KV19 is open to the public but KV5 is not.

Prisons – the prison in Luxor is in Medina Street. The large prisons are in Cairo but prisoners can get sent to various parts of the country. Prison regime is harsh and, under the old regime, physical and sexual abuse was rife. In local prisons, families often bring food in for imprisoned family members. When several members of one family are arrested and held at the prison, it is often stormed by relatives attempting to free them. (See Callabouche.)

Prostitution – there are female prostitutes in Luxor but most visitors would not be aware of them. There are, however, many male prostitutes working the Corniche who cater for the needs of older women (gigolos) and gay men (rent boys).

Ptah – was one of the earliest major deities with his cult centre at Memphis. He was the god of craftsmen and architects and was part of a triad as the husband of Sekhmet and the father of Nefertum. He was greatly revered in Luxor and became one of Ramses II's four great Gods at Abu Simbel. (Ra, Amun, Ptah and Ramses himself). In some creation theories Ptah is credited with the creation of Ra. He is shown in mummified form with a skull cap and carrying a sceptre.

Ptolemy – Ptolemy was one of Alexander the Great's generals who took Egypt as his share of the spoils following the death of

Alexander in 323 BCE. He established himself on the throne as Ptolemy I and founded a dynasty that lasted for 300 years. All of the male Ptolemaic Pharaohs were called Ptolemy and some continued the tradition of building temples to Egyptian gods. The Temple of Isis at Philae, the Hathor Temple at Dendera and the Horus Temple at Edfu are excellent examples. Cleopatra VII was the last Ptolemy Pharaoh as her son Caesarion by Julius Caesar was assassinated when she committed suicide following Octavian's conquest of Egypt in 30 BCE. There are relatively few Ptolemaic monuments in Luxor but there is the delightful temple to Hathor at Deir el Medina and some late additions at the front of Medinet Habu. There is also a shrine to Alexander's immediate successor, Philip Arrhidaeus (King of Macedonia) in Karnak Temple.

Public Telephones – there are public telephone kiosks belonging to a variety of companies throughout Luxor and at 'Central' which houses the main offices of Egypt Telecom in Temple Karnak Street. Coins can be used in them but pre-paid cards are easier and can be bought at most pharmacies and mobile phone shops.

Public Toilets – are generally to be avoided. Use hotel toilets if you have an emergency. Carry some tissues in your bag. Public toilets on trains are acceptable when the journey first starts but quickly deteriorate as time progresses; again there will be no toilet paper.

Puddleduck Restaurant – is a recommended British-run restaurant with a constantly changing menu. It is in Medina Street just past the end of St, Joseph's Street.

Pylon – in Europe, pylons are huge metal structures that are strung with power lines and march across the countryside. In architecture they are the enormous gateways of Egyptian temples. They were called pylons because of their shape which resembled the Greek letter pi. Many pylons are intricately decorated with the accomplishments of the Pharaoh to whom it is dedicated. They are plain stone now but were originally richly coloured.

Pyramids – although it may come as a surprise to Hollywood film producers, the big pyramids are in Giza and Saqqara not in Luxor although there are small pyramid structures to be found in the Deir el Medina. Although the Pharaohs of the New Kingdom had long since abandoned the idea of building pyramids, (as they were too costly in terms of finance, time and labour), the pyramid shape, by resembling the rays of the sun, continued to hold significance. The mountain ('Qurn') could have been instrumental in the Pharaohs choosing the Valley of the Kings as a final resting place. In Luxor, the deceased is not buried inside the structure but in an underground chamber in front of it. The Pyramid of Khufu (named Cheops by the Greeks) at Giza is the largest pyramid and is the only one of the Seven Wonders of the Ancient World that still exists. Satellite imagery is revealing the sites of several previously unknown pyramids around Saqqara where the famous step pyramid is situated. Despite fantasy theories that they might have been built by aliens, there are sufficient examples in the north to show that the ancient Egyptians had many unsuccessful attempts at building pyramids before they got it right.

A Mud Brick House in Old Qurna

Q

Qabawi – Qus

Qabawi – is an area to the north of Luxor, on the West Bank, which has been quite strongly developed in recent years and is the site of the new village (Qurna Gedida) that was built to house the people moved from the Theban Hills following the clearance of the houses there.

Qena – lies to the north of Luxor about an hour's journey away by car. There is a bridge there leading from the east to the west bank so most people travelling west to Abydos or east to Hurghada will pass through the town en route to their destination. Luxor was once part of Qena Governorate but is now a Governorate in its own right. There is much more heavy industry in Qena than in Luxor and it is not dependent on tourism. Comparatively, it is cleaner and better cared for than Luxor is.

Qift - is a small town on the road to Qena, with remains of an important temple to the god Min, who was later identified with Amun as Amun-Min. The men of Qift were taught and used by early Egyptologists in their excavations. Their aptitude having been passed down the generations, to this day, they still form a substantial part of the skilled teams working on the West Bank.

Quad-Biking – early morning quad-biking sessions can be booked through a company that operates in the new buildings close to the west bank ferry point - (opposite the Nile Valley Hotel). There is a quad bike usually parked outside their offices. This could be thrilling but remember that it is classed as a dangerous sport so check your insurance before you sign up for the experience.

Queens – the most famous Queens in Thebes's history are Hatshepsut, Nefertari and Nefertiti, although there were other Queens who wielded great influence. Each Pharaoh had a principal wife, several lesser wives and a substantial harem. It was the principal wife that is now referred to as 'Queen' although this term was not used at the time. It was her eldest surviving son that usually became heir to the throne. The multiplicity of wives and potential heirs without doubt contributed to the fall of the New Kingdom dynasties. Ramses III is thought to have died in a harem plot hatched by one of his minor Queens who aimed to put her son on the throne. The Valley of the Queens lies at the southern end of the Theban Hills and tickets can be bought at the gate. Admission is 30 LE.

Quizzes – pub type quizzes are regularly held at the Regal Lounge in Medina Street, Pub 2000 and occasionally at the Gaddis Hotel in Khaled Ibn el Walid Street.

Qur'an – (Koran) is the sacred book of Muslims which was delivered to Mohammed and is considered as the direct word of Allah. The Qur'an (The Message) was delivered to Mohammed over a period of 23 years and consists of 114 chapters (surahs) of unequal length. The first surah of the Koran, the al fatiha, is used extensively in prayer and is broadcast from the mosques.

Qurn - the 'horn' is the highest point on the Theban Hills standing at 420 metres. The Qurn is associated with both Hathor and with Meretseger. The peak can be reached from the Valley of the Kings or from the Deir el Medina. Wear good shoes if you intend to make the climb and remember to take water with you.

Qurna – is not really a town or a village; it is a fairly large west bank area made up of several villages that spreads several kilometres either side of the crossroad checkpoint leading from the ferry. The centre of the 'village' is close to the temple of Seti I, and has a large local hospital, and a wide variety of shops. Old Qurna was a settlement on and around the tombs of the Nobles, and was demolished in 2010, the inhabitants being moved to the new town near Qabawi.

Qurna Gedida – is the new village which was built near Qabawi to rehouse the people who were moved from the Theban Hills. They were squatters who had built their houses above the tombs of various ancient dignitaries and the government, fearing illegal digging and tomb robbing, had been trying, without success, to demolish the houses for sixty years. Amid great controversy, they had to move in with bulldozers to accomplish their task. There are mixed feelings over the new houses but women tend to like them as they have piped water and sanitation which the old houses lacked.

Qus – is close to Luxor but is part of Qena Governorate. There is little left of the temple of Horus the Elder which once stood there. The town is now part of a major project to turn sugar cane waste into paper.

The Ramesseum

R

Ra – Rubbish

Ra – is a solar deity; the creator sun god who in one myth rose from the Ogdoad egg at Medinet Habu. All forms of life are thought to have been created by Ra who called them into being through knowledge of their real names. He was worshipped from very early times and in the New Kingdom era was fused with Amun to become Amun-Ra and the king of all the gods. He was in conflict with Isis who tricked him into revealing his real name, giving her the power to restore Osiris's life. He is the father of Sekhmet, and of Hathor, although she is sometimes listed as his wife.

Rabbits –are known as 'aanab' and are raised for food. They are bought live from the markets and eaten when they are still small.

Rabies – is endemic in Africa and is present in Luxor. If you are bitten by an animal seek medical help immediately so that tests can be done and treatment started.

Rain – rain is infrequent in Luxor and averages only 1 mm per year. However, violent rain storms occur every few years and can cause devastation when the mud brick houses collapse. There is no street drainage but there are now storm drains in place on the west bank.

Ramadan – is a month long time of fasting and celebration. Fasting lasts between dawn and dusk and the celebrations start as the sun sets. Iftar (breakfast – breaking the fast - which is held at sunset) is often preceded by something sweet such as dates. The start of the Ramadan Festival is not static but, being based on a Lunar Calendar, moves forward by 12 days each year. In 2012 Ramadan was in July and the intense heat coupled with lack of water caused many health problems. It will also occur in the heat of summer in 2013. The Koran does not expect young children to fast but some misguided parents encourage their children to do so as they think it is noble whereas it is extremely harmful.

Several Luxor cafes that serve alcohol at other times will not do so during Ramadan.

Rameseum – is the mortuary temple of Ramses II in the west bank necropolis. It was meant to be his 'temple of a million years', but was built close to the floodplain, so that its foundations were gradually undermined, resulting in severe damage. It is now largely in ruins but many of the columns from the hypostyle hall are still standing and are certainly worth seeing. The temple is atmospheric and is home to the colossal fallen statue of Ramses II which prompted the poet Shelley (who had never seen it) to write the poem Ozymandias. The mud brick vaults that surround the temple have recently been extensively restored and there is talk of raising and then renovating the fallen statue. The temple was dedicated to Amun and to Ramses himself.

Ramla – means 'sand' and is used to refer to the area of new buildings close to the ferry on the west bank which were built on a sand bank.

Ramses I – was the first Pharaoh of the Ramesside dynasties. He was a soldier and not of royal birth. His reign was extremely short and there are no major buildings dedicated to him. His tomb is small compared with later tombs and that of his son Seti I but is worth visiting as it is well decorated. He did not have time to build a mortuary temple of his own but Seti I dedicated a part of his own mortuary temple to his father. Ramses's mummy was discovered in a side show near the Niagara Falls in Canada and was returned to Luxor Museum with full honours in 2003. He was succeeded by his son Seti.

Ramses II – was the son of Seti I and the 3rd Pharaoh of the 19th dynasty. He is described as the greatest and most powerful of all the Egyptian Pharaohs. Few people in history have been awarded the title of 'Great' but he is among those honoured. He held the throne of Egypt for more than 60 years and although his military successes might be exaggerated, he was a formidable foe. He was buried in an ill-sited tomb in the Valley of the Kings which suffered from frequent flooding and was silted up but his mummy was moved to a secret cache by the priests of Amun and then was rediscovered in 1881. It is now in Cairo museum. His mortuary temple (Ramesseum – temple of a million years) was equally ill-sited and also flooded regularly but is atmospheric and well worth visiting to see the fallen statue and the remains of the hypostyle hall. He was a prolific builder, not just of temples but of a whole new city in the north. There are colossal statues of him in both Luxor and Karnak Temples and at Abu Simbel in the south and Memphis in the north. He had many wives, his favourite being Nefertari, and a large number of children. He was succeeded by his 13th son Merenptah.

Ramses III – was the son of Setnahkt and a 20th dynasty Pharaoh who reigned for around 30 years but most of his reign was beset with strife from persistent invasions from the Sea Peoples and the Libyans. Constant wars depleted the treasury and led to internal strife that ultimately led to the collapse of the 20th dynasty and the end of the so called New Kingdom. He was also a prolific builder and his mortuary temple (Medinet Habu) has some wonderful reliefs. Learning from the past and seeing how easily the feats of previous Pharaohs could be obliterated or usurped, the carvings in his temple are particularly deep. The Osiris courtyard that he had constructed at Karnak Temple is superb. It is accepted that he did not meet a natural death and was thought to have fallen victim to a harem plot and been poisoned but close examination of his mummy, (which is held in Cairo Museum), has shown a deep cut on his throat so he may have been killed in this way. He was succeeded by his son Ramses IV. His tomb has been open since antiquity and is one of the largest in the Valley of the Kings (KV11). His exquisitely decorated sarcophagus is in the Louvre museum.

Ramses Station – is Cairo's main rail terminal. It is in neo-Moorish style and was built in 1892 on the site of an older terminal. It was upgraded in 1955 and upgraded again in 2011/2012. It serves as a terminal for all trains going west along the coast to Alexandria as well as those going south to Luxor. A huge statue of Ramses II, which was found in 1820 at Memphis, used to stand outside the station but this was moved in 2006 to the site which will become the new Grand Egyptian Museum.

The same advice is offered for buying tickets to Luxor that relates to buying tickets to Cairo. (See 'Stations'.) There are a limited number of tickets to each station so if tickets to Luxor have all been sold then ask for a ticket to Aswan, it will not cost much more and seats might still be available.

Rape – of both men and women does occur but is not frequent and is largely unreported. There have been reports of male prisoners being raped after arrest as a method of intimidation and male tourists have been raped in the sugar cane after propositioning boys. Rape of Egyptian women is more often abuse from a family member than from a stranger as they are seldom out of the house alone. Rape of European women does occur but this is mainly where a woman has let the situation get to a point where the male will no longer take 'no' for an answer. Female tourists should not leave themselves vulnerable by being alone with men they are only acquainted with as this is often misunderstood as an invitation. If a woman is alone with a workman, she should leave the door open so that there can be no misunderstanding. In Islam, there is a saying that a man and a woman are never alone as the devil is there with them. Women are often held to blame when they are raped for putting themselves in a situation where it could occur. There is no such thing as 'marital rape' in Egyptian law and the police are reluctant to get involved in any case that involves assault by a spouse.

Rats – Luxor has rather of a lot 'feran' – 'big mice' – which do not appear to bother the local population as much as they bother Europeans. The river banks are infested with them and at dusk they can be seen darting about close to the ferry areas. Rat traps can be bought in any of the local markets. Although the traps are humane and do not kill the animal it is common practice to kill all rats when caught as it is considered unfair to release the rat and make it someone else's problem. They are of the brown rat species but are actually grey in colour.

Red Sea – runs along the eastern edge of mainland Egypt and divides it from the Sinai Peninsula. It has an outlet to the Indian Ocean and is joined to the Mediterranean Sea through the Suez Canal. Egypt has several resorts on the mainland (Hurghada,

Safaga, Marsa Alam) and on the peninsula (Sharm el Sheikh, Dahab). The parting of the Red Sea features prominently in the bible story of the Exodus of the Jews from Egypt. Its mainland resorts can be reached by road from Luxor and there are direct flights from Luxor to Hurghada and Sharm el Sheikh.

Reincarnations – there are a lot of 'reincarnations' in Luxor. Most are female and they vary from being Temple Dancers to Queens such as Nefertari and Nefertiti. Although there was only one Nefertari she appears to be able to split her mystic self between half a dozen reincarnations at any one time and the Temple Dancers have seldom passed on their skill. I have yet to meet anyone who claims to be a reincarnated domestic skivvy or ordure shoveller. (See Om Seti.)

Rent Boys – work the Corniche late at night often with an opening gambit of "you need felucca" or "you want I help you" often accompanied by suggestive movements and rubbing of the crotch area. This is mainly as a result of poverty as the boys are not usually gay and are seldom submissive. It is seen as a job and a means of feeding the family. In succumbing to temptation you run the risk of being caught 'in flagrante', embarrassed and possibly deported. There is a very real risk of being robbed or finding yourself in a very costly 'honey-trap' situation. Blackmail is common. Remember that photos are now easily taken on mobile phones.

Renting Property – renting property in Luxor is easy but landlords who rent to Europeans can have a tendency to be obtrusive and can turn up at all times of the night and day especially if the tenant is female and alone. Renting can give you a freedom that is not found in hotels but rent through a registered agency who can deal with problems for you.

Repairmen – it is possible to get just about anything repaired in Luxor as long as it does not need a spare part but locals seldom repair anything. If something breaks it generally stays broken but stays in the same spot to be admired. However, repairmen such as plumbers, electricians, painters and carpenters will happily come to your home to repair things for you. Unfortunately they seldom have their own tools and will be reliant on the screwdrivers, spanners and hammers in your toolbox. They also work on their own sense of timescale and you may have to wait days for them to turn up even in an emergency.

Resorts – there are no tourist resorts in Luxor as such, but there is a new residential site called Egyptian Experience, that will have swimming pools and restaurants, being developed close to the bridge. The Sofitel Karnak, the Jolie Ville and Hilton hotels class themselves as resorts, due to their extensive grounds and facilities

Restaurants – there is a wealth of eating opportunities in Luxor catering for all tastes. For Egyptian food the Sofra and Om Hashim restaurants can be recommended. For English food, it is hard to beat The Lantern or the Old Winter Palace.

Rice – ('ruz')is the staple diet of Egyptians and is cooked in many ways. Care must be taken when eating rice in restaurants though as it is a breeding ground for bacteria. Rice in restaurants is seldom thrown away and is added to constantly at a temperature which is warm rather than hot and is a common source of food poisoning.

Ritual Cleansing – ('tahara') in Islam washing is mandatory before prayer. It takes two forms; the lesser cleansing ('wudu') is done to remove grime and basically involves the washing of face, hands and feet; the greater cleansing ('ghusl') is performed after sex and at the end of a menstrual periods and involves washing the whole body including hair. Menstrual periods are considered unclean and women are not allowed to pray or enter a mosque while menstruating or bleeding following childbirth.

Rosetta Stone – the temples and tombs in Luxor are covered with hieroglyphs which meant little until they could be deciphered. The key to deciphering the hieroglyphs was in the Rosetta Stone. The stone was engraved with the same information in three different languages and from that it was possible for Jean Francois Champollion to compare the scripts and decipher them. The stone was carved in Memphis but was later moved to the town of Rosetta where it was insignificant enough to be used as building material. The stone is now in the British Museum and Egypt has been asking for its return since 2003 but there is a replica in the entrance of the Egyptian Museum in Cairo.

Roundabouts – the traffic rules governing roundabouts in Egypt differs from many other countries as right of way is given to someone joining the roundabout and not to someone already on it.

Rowing Club – is a new building on the southern end of the Corniche. It looks as though it is laid out as a coffee shop. However there is little evidence of activity and no evidence of rowing. Older guide books make reference to an annual rowing festival in Luxor but this has not been held for many years.

Royal Mummies – although the Valley of the Kings was selected for its remoteness and security, the royal tombs proved irresistible for tomb robbers and some were entered many times. By the end of the late 20th dynasty many of the tombs had been looted and the mummies of their owners desecrated in the search for the amulets that were hidden in their wrappings. In order to preserve the bodies of their kings, the priests of Amun decided to collect the pathetic remains, re-bandage them as best they could and then hide them in two obscure tombs where they lay undiscovered until the 19th century. One of these caches of royal mummies was discovered by the Abd el Rassuls, a notorious family of local tomb-robbers but several mummies had been disposed of before their activities were stopped. The remaining mummies were moved to Cairo museum where they now lie in specially designed air-tight cases. The mummy of Queen Hatshepsut has recently been identified and may soon join them. The mummy of Ramses I had found its way onto the market in the 1800s and was eventually located in a side show in Canada. It was returned to Egypt with full honours and is now in Luxor museum along with the mummy of Ahmose I the founder of the 18th dynasty.

Rubbish – much of Luxor is spoiled by piles of uncollected rubbish and litter which is liberally dumped by local residents without any concern for its effect on the environment or tourists' perceptions of the town. There are orange collection bins but these are usually piled high and spilling over with rubbish long before they are emptied. The Amun street cleaners only tend to the major thoroughfares. Household rubbish is simply dumped in plastic bags by the side of the road where it is left to rot. Often the bags are torn open by animals or deliberately torn open to feed goats. The banks of the canals are often covered with discarded rubbish which fouls the water and exacerbates the rat problem. Egypt is facing far greater problems than rubbish disposal following the revolution but hopefully this is something that Luxor Supreme Council will tackle and education programmes may eventually help solve.

Entrance to the Souk

S

Sacred Lakes – Swimming

Sacred Lakes – many early Asian religions as well as the Egyptian religions had sacred lakes in their temples and used water in their rituals. The sacred lakes in the temples in Luxor were set close to the temple or within its precincts and represented the world before time began. The water in the lake was used for ritual cleansing and for sacred rites. Most of the lakes are now dry but Karnak's sacred lake is impressive and there are remains of a sacred lake at Medinet Habu. Until the mud brick wall of the Medinet Habu temple was restored in the 1970s, local women would walk around the lake seven times in the hope of becoming pregnant.

Saint George - ('Mar Girgis') is greatly revered in the Coptic faith and there is a pilgrimage to the monastery at Armant every year which is attended by more than a million people from all over Egypt. Images of St. George in the monastery and in Luxor's Coptic churches show him dressed in mediaeval metal armour not in Egyptian clothing. There is a celebration of St. George in the Coptic churches on 23rd April which is also celebrated as St. George's day in the UK. Girgis is a common name in Luxor's Coptic community.

Saint Joseph Street – is the street which runs from the St. Joseph Hotel in Khaled Ibn el Walid Street through to Medina Street. Its real name is El Mahdi Street.

Saint Mary's Cathedral – (Santa Maria) is the main place of Coptic worship in Luxor and is situated in Temple Karnak Street. It has recently celebrated its 100th anniversary but before the revolution was in grave danger of being demolished to make room for the restoration of the Avenue of Sphinxes between Luxor and Karnak Temples. The interior is splendid and visitors are welcome.

Salah-al-Din – took on the Crusaders in the 12th century and built the Citadel on Cairo's highest point to protect the city from invaders. He is still greatly revered with several Luxor schools and streets named after him.

Salt – there is often far too much salt in food to suit European tastes and salads can be rendered inedible by its over-use. If you want something prepared without salt make it clear when ordering. In Arabic 'mafeesh melha' (salt gone) should make it clear. However, some salt is necessary to stay healthy in hot climates.

Sarcophagus – literally means 'corpse eater' and is the name given to the outer stone casing which holds a coffin and gave added protection to body inside. It was generally meant to be shown above ground or in a tomb rather than being buried and, in the royal tombs, some of the sarcophagi are huge and weigh several tonnes. Some are plain limestone or granite but others are skilfully decorated with texts about the life of the deceased and images of the goddesses Isis and Nephthys. The massive broken sarcophagus inside the tomb of Merenptah has recently been reconstructed and can now be admired as the tomb has been reopened to the public.

Satellite TV – there are several free English-language film channels on NileSat and HotBird satellite systems. MBC2, Fox Movies, AlnaharMov, Top Movies and Panorama Action all have good reception and show fairly recently released films. In addition, Fox, Fox FX, MBC Max, MBC Action, MBC Persia, MBC4 and Dubai One all show English language programmes. You might need to do a bit of channel hopping to find what suits you. Most hotels have Satellite TV in their rooms.

Savoy Street – is the two-level shopping arcade which starts alongside the offices of Luxor Supreme Council on the Corniche and runs through to Karnak Temple Street. Although it was built relatively recently following the demolition of the old souk, it has not worn well and the restaurants that moved there have been struggling.

SCA – Supreme Council of Antiquities – was established in 1858 and is responsible for the care and maintenance of all of Luxor's antiquities. Since January 2011 the SCA has been an independent ministry and the name was changed to Ministry of State for Antiquities (MSA).

Scams – there are too many scams operating in Luxor to list them all here, just as there are in all tourist resorts throughout the world and, although it is hard to believe, conmen have actually sold Luxor Temple to tourists on several occasions. In Thailand people can be conned over gem stones, in London people can be conned over expensive theatre tickets, in Luxor people can be conned over love as the biggest scams appear to be operated through the gigolo system. Naive tourists fall for undying-love declarations and part with all their savings to invest in property which they never own and start businesses which are doomed to failure. Another major scam involves the translation of documents. All important documents or leases need to be translated by an authorised translator in Cairo and not by a friend of a friend. It has been known for a translator to contact the contract's other party and ask them what they want the translation to say. What people think they have and what they actually have are seldom the same. Never put assets of any kind in anyone else's name. You might be told that it will save time and money but it will not; it will merely mean that you do not own what you think you have bought and the person who does own it (with your money) is highly unlikely to give it back so you will lose it. This is a certainty not a possibility. One of the simplest scams is about getting change after shopping as trying to get change from someone can be like getting blood from a stone so make sure that you have spare notes in your pocket. Also take into consideration that you could be a target for expat led scams as well as those operated by locals.

Scarabs – the scarab formed the most important amulet in ancient Egypt. A scarab is a dung beetle and not a rapacious flesh-eater as shown in modern day horror films. Ancient Egyptians observed the larvae emerging from dung balls but, not realising that the dung contained scarab eggs, they associated them with miraculous rebirth. Also, an ancient myth had the sun being rolled across the sky by a scarab and it became associated with the sun god Ra. Initially scarabs formed cheap amulets that anyone could afford but later they were ornamented and figured in gold and precious stones. Larger versions of the scarab were placed over the throats, chests or hearts of mummies to protect them. The underside of these scarabs was often inscribed with a prayer to help the deceased in the heart weighing ceremony. Locally, scarabs are carved from a variety of stone and make cheap and attractive souvenirs.

Schools – under Luxor's previous administration there was a plan to move all the east bank schools to a site along Television Street but the plan appears to have been shelved. Children should start school when they are six years old and education is mandatory but attendance is not enforced so few children from very poor families attend school. Classes can be very large with up to 70 children in them.

Scorpions – there are many scorpions on the west bank but they are not of the most virulent variety. Their stings are very painful and although they are unlikely to kill an adult they can make children and the elderly very ill. All pharmacies carry the anti-venom and it is wise to have this injected as soon as possible after being stung. If you are in a village then someone may take you to a sheikh for treatment. If so then be careful as he is likely to cut the area and attempt to suck out the venom. This in itself is not that harmful but unfortunately the razor blade used to make the cut is used time and time again and Hep C is rife in Egypt.

Secrets – ancient Egypt was steeped in secrets and mysteries held by a very powerful priesthood who guarded them closely. They ranged from the daily resurrection of the sun through to the rites of the Book of the Dead which gives the secrets and spells for gaining an Afterlife. Sorcery, magic and rituals governed many aspects of life but the secrets leaked out and by the late New Kingdom such secrets were being openly bought and sold.

Security – under the old regime security in Egypt was very tight but it lapsed alarmingly following the 2011 'revolution'. Violence does still flare periodically but on the whole Egypt is once again secure and is a safe destination for tourists, although there are always sensationalist reports in the media when demonstrations are held in Cairo. In Luxor, police and many of the guards in the temples are armed but this is done discretely and is done only for tourists' safety.

Sekhmet – is a warrior goddess and accompanied the Pharaohs into battle. She was fierce and her breath is thought to have created Egypt's deserts. She is shown as a lioness with a sun disc and Uraeus on her head. She was considered as the daughter of Ra, the wife of Ptah and the mother of Nefertum the lotus god. There are statues of her in several Luxor temples. Most of them show her in a seated position but a standing statue was recently unearthed in the Temple of Mut at Karnak.

Senegal Thick Knee – is a wading bird of medium size that can be seen on the islands in the river. It likes open ground near water and takes its name from its large prominent knees.

Serpents – there are snakes in Luxor and some of them are venomous but few are large enough to be classed as serpents. There are two significant serpents in Egyptian mythology. The serpent shown on the headdresses of various Pharaohs and gods is called a Uraeus and the huge serpent shown on the walls of temples and tombs is Apophis – the embodiment of all evil.

Service Cars – locally known as arabeya, are the main means of travel for Egyptians in Luxor. The minibuses run in loops around the town for 24 hours with a fare of 50 piastras. The old 'hantour' converted trucks on the west bank are gradually being replaced by minibuses. Fuel shortages and reduced fuel subsidies are bound to lead to increased fares.

Seth – is brother of Osiris and Isis and husband of his sister Nephthys. He had a particularly violent birth and although worshipped from very early times was always associated with evil. The legend of his fraternal fight with Osiris endures. Seth murdered his brother and dismembered his body, sending parts to all corners of Egypt. Osiris was restored by their sister Isis but enmity between the two brothers still continued until there was a fight between Seth and Osiris's son Horus which left one emasculated and the other blind. Seth does have a redeeming feature in that he accompanied the solar boat through the underworld and spears the serpent Apophis which allows the boat to progress on its journey and let the new day begin.

Seti I – was the son of Ramses I and the father of Ramses the Great. He expanded the Egyptian empire to include Cyprus and parts of Mesopotamia. He was a prolific builder and his masterpieces are the Temple of Osiris at Abydos and additions to Karnak Temple. His tomb in the Valley of the Kings is one of the most spectacular but is in a precarious condition and has been closed to the general public for many years. There are many reliefs of his exploits on the outside of the northern part of Karnak's hypostyle hall.

Seti I, Temple of – the mortuary temple of Seti I is set slightly away from the rest of the temples and is close to the cemetery in the El Genena village area of Qurna near the Carter House and the beginning of the road to the Valley of the Kings. Tickets need to be bought at the ticket office. The pylons of the temple are largely ruined as they were made from mud brick but the main temple is remarkably intact and there are some fine reliefs. There is a Nilometer in the temple precinct. An area of the temple is dedicated to Seti's father, Ramses I, as he did not have time to build a temple for himself. The temple was dedicated to Amun and was used for worship but it also served as a treasury and, as the temple was unfinished at the time of Seti's death, it was finished by his son Ramses II.

Sexually Transmitted Diseases – Egypt has a growing problem with sexually transmitted diseases of all types even though it is a Muslim country. The low use of condoms exacerbates the problem and shame leads to many cases remaining untreated and the disease is passed on. If participating in a sexual relationship it is vital to protect yourself as many gigolos swear that they are virgins even though they lost count of their conquests long ago.

Shabaan – is a common name among men in Luxor and is also the name of the Islamic month preceding Ramadan.

Shabti – are dolls that look like mummies. They can be made of wood, clay or faience and would be found in tombs. Their purpose is to act as servants to the deceased. They carry the tools of their trade so a gardener shabti would carry a hoe or perhaps a basket. You can buy replicas in the souk but be careful that they are known to be replicas as some people have been stopped at Luxor airport and accused of smuggling antiques.

Shahadah – is the declaration that 'there is no god apart from God, and Mohammed is the Messenger of God". This simple statement, said with belief, makes a person a Muslim.

Sharia – is Arabic for street or pathway.

Sharmoota – is Arabic for 'prostitute' and is often used as an insult by irate motorists venting road rage at pedestrians and other road users.

Shawarma – beef or chicken shawarma makes a very tasty meal. It is comprised of spiced shredded meat or chicken with peppers and onions fried in oil and served in a rich tomato sauce. It is usually accompanied with rice but can be obtained with 'chips' or in a roll as a sandwich.

Sheep – along with goats can be found all over Luxor both in the villages and in town. Many are bred for slaughtering at the Eid el Adha festival and sometimes a whole sheep is cooked and given to the poor to bless a new venture. In town, they can mainly be seen shortly after dawn when the shepherd drives them along the streets tearing open rubbish bags for them to eat any discarded food. They are housed on rooftops as well as on spare ground.

Sheherazade Hotel – is a modern hotel, on the West Bank, in Gezera village.

Sheikh – is an Islamic scholar who often acts as an advisor settling family problems and local disputes. He does not need to be attached to a mosque. There is also another kind of 'sheikh', who would more accurately be described as a shaman although he would never be called that, from whom people buy papers and potions to counteract 'bad-eyes' and to lift spells that have been cast by enemies or to cast spells on rivals.

Sheraton Hotel – is a 5* chain hotel at the end of Khaled Ibn el Walid Street.

Sherif al Rhoda Street - is known as Little Britain Street and runs from opposite the Sonesta Hotel in Khaled Ibn el Walid Street through to Medina Street. A fixed-price Government shop is on a corner of the Medina Street end. There are several English style restaurants in the street.

Shish Kebab – Shish Kebab is skewers of grilled beef/lamb with additions of onions/tomatoes/peppers depending on the restaurant.

Shish Tawouk – Shish Tawouk is identical to Shish Kebab but with chunks of chicken instead of meat.

Shisha – is also commonly known as a 'hookah'. As it is a male social activity, you will see men smoking shishas in all of the outdoor coffee shops. A shisha is a device where the smoke from flavoured tobaccos is drawn through water to cool the smoke. Due to the length of time that is taken over smoking the shisha, the health dangers are considered to be the same as smoking up to 60 cigarettes.

Shoes – sandals are quite adequate for most of the time in Luxor but it is better to wear more sensible shoes when you know you will be walking over rough ground or descending into the tombs. Shoes are worn in towns but in the villages many adults and most children are shoeless and barefooted.

Shoe-Shine Boys – there are many shoe-shine boys in Luxor who will badger you to have your shoes cleaned even if you are wearing strap sandals. Too many of them are still children and should be in school but their families are probably dependent on the small amount of money that they earn. The youngest I have seen was a small girl of about four years old who worked outside the Winter Palace Hotel. She probably earned a lot from sympathy tips but was actually in great danger from abuse.

Shokran – is Arabic for 'thank you'. 'Shokran gezeelan' is 'thank you very much'.

Shuft – is Arabic for 'I saw' and was brought back to the UK by returning soldiers as slang for 'have a look' – 'have a shuftee'.

Shura – Luxor has two elected members of the Shura Council which is the Upper Legislative House of the Egyptian Government.

SIM Cards – if your mobile phone is not locked into a system, buying a local SIM card will save you a lot of money in phone calls. They are cheap (approximately 10 LE) and freely available. Legally, retailers have to take your identification details and will ask for your passport so get it copied or give an Egyptian a small sum to get a SIM card for you. A Holiday SIM card (25 LE) has a 4 week life, but gives cheaper rates for calls than a normal one. Most of the mobile phone companies offer a variety of tariffs and they work out very much cheaper than roaming rates.

Sindbad's – is a favourite expat watering hole. It is quiet and does serve beer (but not during Ramadan). It is situated on the forecourt of the old Wena Luxor Hotel and is rumoured to be ready for closure when the hotel renovations progress.

Singers – Egyptians love to sing and there are shops selling tapes and CDs spread about the town. When there is a shop opening or a wedding, music blares out of loud speakers for hours. The most popular Egyptian born singers are Amr Diab, Mohamed Mounir, Om Khalthoum, Hisham Abbas, Tamar Hosni, and Shereen Wagdi.

Skin Lighteners – sadly many young women believe that they will be more attractive and have a better life if they had lighter skin. Television adverts showing models being rejected for the best jobs until they have bleached their skin by plastering their faces with 'Fair and Lovely' makes the problem worse. Skin lighteners may no longer contain the toxic compounds they use to have but they still lead to skin complaints and the adverts may cause low self-esteem in girls who cannot afford the 'treatments'.

Snack Time – is a fast food outlet close to Luxor Temple. It is clean and bright and its food is tasty. There is a wonderful view of the temple from the upper floors and there is a free Wi-Fi Internet connection. They have a home delivery service.

Snakes – 34 different varieties of snake have been identified in Egypt most of them harmless but there are venomous cobras and hooded vipers. The 'snake man' is called in to remove snakes when they are sighted but is unlikely to do himself out of further business by catching them all. Meretseger was the goddess who protected the tomb workers from snakes and scorpions.

Snobs Restaurant – is an English style restaurant with an Egyptian owner and is a firm favourite in Luxor. The menu is mixed and the service acceptable. It is situated in Sherif el Rhoda Street.

Soap Sagas – soap sagas with Egyptian themes, past and present, proliferate on Egyptian television and are avidly watched, particularly during Ramadan.

Sobek - is the crocodile god much favoured by the Greeks. There is a Ptolemaic temple to Sobek at Kom Ombo which is to the south of Luxor and easily reached by road.

Sofitel Hotel – is a 5* resort-type hotel on the outskirts of Luxor beyond Karnak.

Sofra Restaurant – is a very atmospheric Egyptian style restaurant set in an old villa in a side street off Manshia Street

(Twinky Street). It is signposted and offers good food at reasonable prices in a romantic setting. Worth a visit but avoid the roof in the winter months as it can be very chilly.

Sonesta St George Hotel – is a 5* hotel about halfway along Khaled Ibn el Walid Street.

Sons of Horus – the fatherhood of the four sons of Horus is questionable and credited to several gods but is generally accepted to be Horus with Isis, his own mother, as their mother. They, (Imsety, Hapy, Duamutef and Kebehsenuef), are funerary deities and appear regularly in tomb paintings but do not appear to have any temples or cults attached to them. Each of the four canopic jars was dedicated to the respective son that was responsible for a particular organ. Most bazaars sell canopic jars made from resin or carved from a variety of stone and they make excellent souvenirs but make sure you get the set of four with the different heads on the lids. - baboon, jackal, falcon and human. (See Canopic Jars)

Souk – the main tourist souk in Luxor has its entrance close to Luxor Temple and is a treasure trove of souvenirs. Be prepared to bargain for everything. The Egyptian souk selling fruit, fish, vegetables, shoes and clothes follows on from the tourist souk after it crosses El Hussain Street by the Venus Hotel.

Sound and Light Show – is held at Karnak Temple and starts soon after sunset every day of the week and is repeated several times each evening. The accompanying dialogue is offered in several languages and the order in which languages are presented changes from day to day and differs between summer and winter, so it is important that you attend the appropriate session to get the best from the show. The times are shown on a board at the ticket office which is at the front and to the right of the temple's entrance. The show gives an atmospheric historic display of the temple and is worth seeing. The Theban hills are also illuminated at night, giving a backdrop to the display. Tickets are 100 LE each with half-price for children and students.

Soup – is known as 'shorba' and most restaurants offer a range on their menus but the local soup is a thin beef and onion broth thickened with what looks like white melon seeds but which is actually pasta.

Souvenirs – papyrus, stone carvings, bags, carpets and needlework items all make excellent souvenirs of Luxor but unfortunately, many of the cheaper items such as sets of pyramids are made in China not Egypt and many of the old skills are being lost. However, it is still possible to get items that support the local economy. Sadly, except for the outlet of the Urban Women's Centre in Karnak, there are no real Fair Trade shops in Luxor although a local charity is considering starting one when the tourist situation improves.

Spells and Superstitions – it is not just the ancient Egyptians that believed in spells as they are still widely used on the west bank where 'papers' can be bought from the local sheikh to remove 'bad eyes', make troublesome people suffer, make others fall under a spell and cause all manner of mischief. Egyptians are very superstitious people with an arcane belief in ghosts and djinns. The local sheikhs on the west bank do quite a trade in remedies for 'bad eyes' (the evil eye) and many people burn offerings when there is sickness in the house. The list of old wives tales that are still believed is extremely long.

Sphinx – is a mythical creature with the body of a lion and the head of a man although many of the sphinxes in Luxor are ram-headed. The sphinx played the role of guardian and the ram-headed sphinxes that lead up to the entrance of Karnak Temple symbolise the fertility of Amun. The Great Sphinx that everyone associates with the image is situated in Giza, close to the Great Pyramids but there are many smaller ones around the Luxor temples. The processional route between Karnak and Luxor was lined with human-headed ones, which are thought to be in the image of the Pharaoh Nectanebo, who added them to the Avenue. There were probably many more in the necropolis as there is a theory that a sphinx lined road led from Hatshepsut's Palace to the Nile.

Spices – the variety of spices available in the souk is overwhelming and it can be hard to identify exactly which one you require when faced with mountains of colourful powders and ground leaves. As well as for cooking, some spices are taken as medicines in the form of tea and the merchants will tell you all sorts of stories about their curative properties in order to achieve a sale. Some of them actually do work. The blue stuff (indigo) that sits in piles is used in the washing process for highlighting the whiteness of clothes. Jars of spices can also be obtained at low cost in the supermarkets.

Sports – Luxor has several Sports Clubs and Football Clubs and has a popular Boxing Club run by an Englishman who is now Luxor's official boxing coach. There is a youth sports centre called the Nasser Club off the Movenpick Road in Awamia.

Stations – ('Mahatta') Luxor train station is very busy with trains travelling north and south. (There are no cross country trains). There is little concept of queuing at the ticket office so you need to be persistent and may have to wield your elbows to stop yourself being pushed further and further back in the 'queue'. There is a strange system of ticket allocation as a certain number of tickets are issued for each stop. So, if all the tickets from Luxor to Cairo have been sold there could still be tickets available from Aswan to Cairo. You do not have to get on the train at Aswan you merely have to pay the extra charge. For security reasons, tourists are restricted over which trains they can travel on. There is a bus station with buses to Hurghada run by Superjet on the right hand side of the train station but the main bus station is near the airport.

Station Street – ('Sharia Mahatta') – runs between the railway station and Luxor Temple. As part of the renovation of Luxor several years ago, the buildings on one side of the street were demolished to widen the road. There is now a clear view of the temple from the train station.

Steam Boats – there are three antique steam boats working on the Upper Nile (Karim, Sudan and Misr – the first two have paddles and the third has a screw) and another working on Lake

Nasser. Several other boats such as the Niagara, Indiana, Fostat and Memnon have been rescued and are awaiting restoration.

Storks – in winter there are many storks travelling through Egypt as they migrate south and they can be seen resting on the islands that form in the Nile. Among them is a less than attractive specimen called the Marabou Stork which looks more than a little dour and is ugly compared with its sleeker relatives. Storks are mute and rely on bill clattering to communicate with each other.

Street Children – Egypt has an immense problem with street children as there are more than one million of them living alone in cities throughout the country. The biggest problem is in Cairo, but there is also a problem in the Luxor area. The Street Children that you see begging in central Luxor are often not always as poverty stricken as they seem as begging can be a business but there are still many who have lost contact with their families and are in desperate need of help.

Student Cards – most of the monuments and tombs accept valid student cards, which give a 50% reduction on ticket costs. The ticket office on the West Bank has a separate window for students. There is also the possibility of reduced rail fares. Student cards can be obtained in Luxor but it is easier to get one before leaving home.

Sugar – Egyptians have a great love of sweet things, almost to the extent of sugar addiction, and have up to six spoonsful of sugar in a small cup of tea. Dietary diabetes has become a great problem. On the Prophet Mohammed's birthday, dolls made of sugar that has been coloured bright pink are offered for sale throughout Luxor.

Sugar Cane – is widely grown in Luxor even though it is a swamp plant, not a desert one. There are several processing plants in the region and a narrow-gauge railway transports the west bank cane to the depot in Armant. Due to constant watering and the consequent raising of the water table, cane crops that are grown near the temples are causing drainage problems and weakening the temples' foundation level of stone.

There are juice bars throughout Luxor that sell freshly crushed sugar cane juice which is greatly favoured by Egyptians of all ages.

Sugaring – is a hair removal system that has been used in Egypt since ancient times. It is an all over body experience used to remove hair from arms, armpits, legs and the pubic area. Traditionally, Egyptian women are 'sugared' to remove all body hair before marriage. This is considered as an excellent alternative to waxing. Sugar compounds can be bought in all local pharmacies but need to be heated to be effective. Whether this is done in the home with a do-it-yourself kit, by a home visitor or by a professional in a salon depends greatly on financial circumstances.

Sunbathing – Luxor does not have any beaches but it does have swimming pools and intense heat so all precautions should be taken when sunbathing to avoid extensive burning. Topless sunbathing is definitely not allowed. Egypt is a Muslim country and its customs should be respected.

Sunshine International Project – it a dual registered (UK and Egypt) charity that has an orphanage for approximately 100 children in a purpose-built centre off the Movenpick Road close to the new Culture Palace. It was started in 1992 by the late Pearl Smith.

Supermarkets – supermarkets are not of the size you find in Europe or in Cairo. Even the large ones are only about the same size as a Tesco Express in the UK but they are well stocked and some carry a range of European foods. Several new ones have recently opened in the Television Street area. There are some very large supermarkets in Cairo but these have yet to reach Luxor.

Supreme Council of Luxor – is responsible for the administration of the whole of Luxor Governorate and is situated on the Corniche next to the El Luxor (Etap) Hotel. The Governor's offices are on the first floor and there is now an appointments system for meeting him.

Sweets – ('helawa') most Egyptians have a sweet tooth and love sweets whatever age they are. When giving sweets to children please do this with dignity and do not throw them and remember that Mum and Granddad would like some too.

Swimming – in the Nile is not recommended as there are strong currents and bilharzia larvae and it is not unusual to find rubbish and the bloated carcasses of animals floating by. Despite this the river is full of fish. Most of the hotels with swimming pools will allow tourists to access them for a small fee. There are many pools on the East Bank ranging from luxury at the Winter Palace to basic at the Shady Hotel in Television Street. On the west bank the Gezera Gardens Hotel, Nile Valley Hotel and El Mesala Hotel all have swimming pools.

Terracotta Pots in the Market

T

Tahina – Twinky Street

Tahina – is made of thick ground paste of sesame seeds. It is an ingredient of most Egyptian salad dressings.

Tamarind – when you are looking at the spice stalls in the souk you may see some strange brown balls of about the same size as a tennis ball. This is dried tamarind. The balls are soaked to make a sweet drink.

Targen – a targen is an unglazed clay cooking pot. Before using, it needs to be treated with salt/oil and fired to make it waterproof. Anything that can be casseroled can go into it. When you see targen on a menu it will be an oven-baked meat, chicken, fish or vegetable casserole.

Tarif - is a village that lies to the north of the necropolis area and has a group of minor undecorated tombs some of which are quite large. Several are actually lived in and are hard to detect as they have been built on and become part of the village.

Taste of India Restaurant – is owned by an Englishman. It has received some good reviews from those who love Indian food and is situated in St. Joseph Street.

Tattoos – in Egypt tattoos are not generally done with a needle but are elaborate applications of Henna dye. It is a custom in several cultures for a bride to have temporary henna tattoos on her hands and the soles of her feet. These are popular with tourists but can take several hours to complete. Some skin is very sensitive to henna and should be tested before applying it to a large area. Copts often have a blue ink tattoo of a cross on the inside of one wrist to denote their religion.

Taxis – are easy to find and, compared with European prices, very cheap to use but Luxor's taxis do not have meters so you need to negotiate the fee. Short journeys cost in the region of 10 LE and a longer one 15 – 20 LE. Naturally the driver may ask for much more. Get out of the taxi when you reach your destination and pay the driver through the window. If he gets abusive and overly demanding, do not get into a heated argument over it, just simply pay him what you think is fair and then walk away.

Tea – Egyptian tea is known as 'chai' and is black. Egyptians like their tea strong, very sweet and without milk or lemon. You are unlikely to come across the mint-tea that is found in other North African countries but you can get it if you ask for it. There is a huge range of packet teas available in the supermarkets. Aniseed tea ('yanseen') tastes good. If you want milk in your tea ('chai bi laban') then make sure that the waiter understands that you want everything served to you separately or you are likely to get a cup of milk with a tea bag in it.

Tea Shops – the nearest thing there is to a European style Tea Shop in Luxor is called Tutti Fruiti in St. Joseph Street. It is owned by an Englishwoman called Christine and sells scones, apple pie etc., plus hot snacks, steak and home-made chips.

Telephone Companies – Egypt Telecom is the operator of the landlines in Egypt and its offices are in Temple Karnak Street. Cards can be obtained to make international calls from land line phones. Vodafone, Mobinil and Etisalat all operate mobile phone services on a contract or pay as you go basis. Their main offices are all on Television Street but there are shops offering phone cards on almost every street.

Televisions – most hotels have televisions, with satellite connections that are pre-programmed for film and news channels, in all rooms. You will find TVs in rented holiday flats too. For buying televisions, there are several shops at the bottom end of Station Street that carry a wide range of styles and screen sizes. Prices are generally slightly higher than in Europe but the new large-screen 3D televisions and very expensive.

Television Street – gets its name from the television mast that thrusts its way above the town. The street has a dual carriageway and is busy with shops on both sides of the road. Be careful when crossing as traffic has a tendency to come at you from all directions. The road was recently extended to link up with the Movenpick Road and it is expected that the land on either side of the extension will be developed which led to a lot of speculative land purchase. The proposal to move Luxor's schools there appears to have been shelved.

Temperatures – in Egypt there is a massive temperature difference between a cold winter night when temperatures plummet and the intense heat of a summer day when temperatures soar. (Egypt's highest temperature of 50°C was recorded at Deir el Bahri in Luxor in the month of May.)

Temples - there are temples on both sides of the river but the most visited ones are Luxor Temple and Karnak Temple on the east bank and Hatshepsut's Temple and Medinet Habu on the west bank. There are two types of temples; those dedicated to local and major gods such as Amun (Luxor and Karnak) and mortuary temples dedicated to the cult of the deceased Pharaoh who was in effect also a god. Most of the temples are in a very poor state of repair or have disappeared altogether but the mortuary temples of Hatshepsut, Seti I, Ramses II and Ramses III are well worth visiting. Some of the temples have deep scrape marks in the outside walls which were caused in ancient times by women scraping off 'holy stone' to mix into a drink that had curative or magical properties.

Terracotta – there is vast array of terracotta items available in the market ranging from small cooking dishes to huge water vats. They are aimed at local people as well as tourists. The terracotta wall lights are particularly attractive. The finish is often crude but they make cheap and useful souvenirs. (See Targen)

Texts – texts do arrive when sent to or from Egypt but the service can be far from immediate and there can be a 24 hour delay in receipt. If something is urgent then telephone and text as a back-up not as a first resort.

Theban Hills – are clearly visible from the east bank and act as a barrier between the green belt of the irrigated area and the endless desert beyond. The highest point is known as the Qurn. For many years the hills were dotted with colourful mud brick buildings but these, amid fears of illegal digging for antiquities and tomb robbing, were controversially demolished and the inhabitants moved to a newly built village ('Qurna Gedida') in 2010. As the sun sets behind the hills it is easy to see why the ancients considered this the gateway to the Afterlife. They are illuminated at night, making a spectacular backdrop to the West Bank.

Thomas Cook – Thomas Cook's association with Luxor is long established and the Thomas Cook offices, having moved from the Winter Palace Hotel, can be found in Khaled Ibn el Walid Street.

Thoth – Thoth is the patron of scribes and is present at the weighing of the heart ceremony to keep records of a person's good and evil acts that are presented to the assessor gods. He is one of the major gods and is shown either in the form of a baboon or as a man with the head of an Ibis. He holds a wand and an ankh. There is a temple to Thoth on the west bank just beyond Medinet Habu and a Sun Temple to him on the heights above the Western Valley.

Threading – is a popular hair removal system that is used by most Egyptian women and by men in the barber shops. It is now being introduced to some European beauty parlours. A twisted strand of thread is manipulated to act as tweezers and effectively removes even the finest hairs from the face. The process involves the use of both hands and of teeth in a three-point system of manipulating the thread. The process is initially very painful but soon drops to an acceptable level.

Tiba- is a new town that is being developed near the airport.

Ticket Offices – the Ticket Office for the west bank monuments is situated past the Colossi of Memnon close to Medinet Habu and you can buy tickets there for most monuments with the exception of the Valley of the Kings, the Valley of the Queens and Deir el Bahri whose tickets ('taskara') can be bought on site. Tickets for Deir el Medina, Seti I, Ramesseum and Carter House have to be bought at the Ticket Office. On the east bank, there is a ticket office at Karnak Temple and another at Luxor Temple. Tickets for the Ptolemaic Temple at El Tod and the tombs at Moalla should be bought at Luxor Temple.

Time – Egyptians are incredibly patient and there is none of the hurry about anything that is found in Europe. This can be very frustrating when you are trying to get something done especially if you are dealing with the authorities. There is no use in shouting or getting angry as it does not speed things along and generally only makes the situation worse. In Egypt 'five minutes' will be nearer to an hour, 'ten minutes' will be all day, 'one hour' will mean tomorrow and 'tomorrow' means next week or another life. Patience is more than a virtue in Egypt, it is a necessity. Time is an irrelevant nuisance invented by foreigners.

Tipping – wages in general are very low and most hotel and restaurant workers are reliant on tips to enhance their wages. Tipping need not be excessive. A small service deserves a small tip of perhaps one Egyptian pound. A large service would be worthy of much more. Some tourists get very concerned about the amount they are giving out in what seems to be endless demands for tips. These are over-generous people who are giving tips when they are not deserved and are being too generous in the amounts that they give each time. Only give a tip when a service has been given and never just because it is demanded. As a rough guide: 10% of the bill is sufficient in an expensive restaurant but 5 LE (which is likely to be far more than 10% of the bill) is the norm in coffee shops. 5 LE is also a sufficient tip for a taxi ride if you feel one has been earned. If someone helps you with your bags in the hotel then, depending on the grade of hotel, anything between 1 LE and 5 LE is acceptable. The same applies to those who help you with your bags at the airport although, as it is their job and there are hundreds of people going through, I would not give more than 1 or 2 LE if there is exceptional service and nothing if there is not. You may also be pushed for tips in shops when you buy something; in this case 5 LE maximum is advised. Larger amounts are more likely to be bribes than tips.

Toilet - there are few public toilets in Luxor and they are not for the faint hearted. If you need to use a toilet then go inside one of the hotels and use their facilities. If you are in a private home and need the toilet expect to find a squatter type toilet instead of a European style one.

Toilet paper - is available in all the supermarkets but is not provided in toilets anywhere other than in the large hotels as the sewage pipes are generally small bore and cannot cope with the paper. For cleanliness, washing facilities are provided via water piped inside the bowl or from an external spray. Paper would be used only to dry the relevant area; the used paper then being placed in a bin. It is advisable to put a few tissues in your bag.

Toiletries – there is no need to waste baggage allowances on bringing toiletries with you on holiday unless you use something special as a wide range of toiletries are stocked by pharmacies and supermarkets. You could leave toiletries behind to be distributed by the local charities but if you do this then please advise the charity concerned otherwise they are unlikely to receive them.

Tomatoes - are grown close to the ground in fields and not strung upwards on wires as they are in Europe. The plants are bushy and the tomatoes grow lush, large and full of flavour.

Tombs – whether it is as a tourist, a tomb-robber or an archaeologist, Egypt's spectacular tombs have always been a source of fascination. In ancient Egypt, anyone who had the funds to organise a funeral that involved more than being tipped into a hole in the ground, would commission a tomb on the western side of the Nile. The west signified the setting sun and was the best place to be interred in the hope of an entrance to the Afterlife which if it could not be achieved through the deceased's own efforts might be achieved vicariously through proximity to the graves of the Pharaohs. Tombs varied from the simple but beautifully decorated workers' tombs in Deir el

Medina, to the more elaborate tombs of the high officials and nobles and then on to the spectacular tombs in the Valley of the Kings and Queens which were final resting places for the royal families. Almost all have been entered and abused in one way or other. Many were robbed almost as soon as they were finished and others were either lived in or used as convenient cattle pens by local farmers but there is no doubt that there are many more tombs still to be discovered. There should be exciting times ahead for Luxor's archaeologists.

Tomb Robbers – when it was found, Tutankhamun's tomb held great treasures, even though he was an undistinguished Pharaoh who died early, but the wealth buried with him was immense. Imagine what the treasures of Ramses II would have been like. The village where the tomb builders lived (Deir el Medina) was well protected from outsiders and the secret position of tombs should have stayed secret but security at times appears to have been as leaky as a sieve. Some tombs were robbed not long after they were completed and others were robbed by later Pharaohs who reused their contents in their own tombs and even usurped their coffins. Tutankhamun's own coffin had been shortened and could have come from another grave. There have always been tomb robbers in Luxor and over the centuries many families have become rich through the illegal sale of artefacts that they have unearthed beneath their homes. Following the 2011 revolution, mass digging spread throughout Egypt as robbers thought they would be able to locate and rob tombs without getting caught. Large tunnels were found in Luxor and arrests were made. Whether or not you think that archaeologists are tomb-robbers depends on your stance. Egypt would say that the archaeologists that removed sacred items from tombs and temples without proper permission and shipped them off to Europe in the 19th century were robbers – and they might be right.

Tomorrow – ('bokra') really does never come in Luxor. When someone says that they will do something for you tomorrow they really mean some time in the distant future. 'Baad Bokra', meaning 'after tomorrow' can be translated as 'in another life'.

Tour Guides – all tour guides are Egyptian and have to pass exams to obtain their cards. Many of them speak several languages and are very knowledgeable about ancient history. However, some only know their speeches by rote and know little beyond the standard guide book information. Apart from the fee charged their main source of income is in taking the client shopping for souvenirs from which he/she will receive around 50% of the money spent.

Tour Leaders – are, at present, almost invariably European as they work for European companies leading European clients but pressure is on to restrict their number following complaints from Egyptians who feel that their job opportunities are being undermined. Leaders are responsible for the safety of their guests and often give out unwarranted warnings of the dire consequences of venturing away from a hotel without them. Like the tour guides they earn most of their income from commissions which their clients are unaware of.

Tourist Information Centre – is across the road from the railway station and offers a good service.

Tourist Police – on the east bank, the Tourist Police used to have their offices on the Corniche but are now situated in a side street to the right of the railway station as you face it. If you have a problem in Luxor involving scams, robbery, violence or sexual assault then report it to them. They are there to help you. However, the standard of English is generally low so you may need an interpreter with you as any statement you make has to be translated into Arabic – and a lot of the facts can get lost in a translation. The system of logging complaints is long and frustrating but it is the only way to get any sort of justice and you must get a police report number for any insurance claim that you might make. Violence is rare but bag snatches, sexual assaults and burglaries have been steadily rising with the lack of policing following the revolution; please report a crime if you are a victim. On the west bank, the Tourist Police offices are adjacent to the Ticket Office and any problems encountered should be reported there.

Touts – all the tourist resorts throughout the world are infested with touts of every description pushing everything from tours, shops and sex through to accommodation and taxi services - although few are as persistent and annoying as those that operate in Luxor. Completely ignoring them is the best way to deal with them except if you are looking for what they are touting.

Traffic – in Luxor is heavy and ill-disciplined. The death rate from traffic accidents is unacceptably high and crossing the road can sometimes be difficult and dangerous. Care needs to be taken at all times. Most vehicles have dents from collisions and few have adequate insurance even though drivers are required to have valid third-party insurance when they tax their cars.

Trains – run north and south but not east or west. There are several trains running daily between Cairo and Aswan but they are not all available to tourists. Tourists are only allowed to travel on the trains which carry security guards. This is done for the safety of the tourist. Time is seldom of essence in Egypt and this applies to trains too so, due to the poor state of the tracks, they seldom run on time and a journey can take much longer than it should. Also, again because of the poor state of the tracks, the safety record is abysmal and there are frequent accidents. The journey from Luxor to Cairo should take between 9 and 10 hours but has been known to take up to 14 hours to complete.

Transferring Funds – at present, the amount of money that you can transfer to Egypt is restricted to around $10,000 in any one transaction. Most banks will make the arrangements for you if you know the SWIFT code of the bank and the account number of the recipient. There is a standard charge for the service regardless of the amount transferred. The alternative is Western Union which has a branch in Television Street. Their charges are percentage based and the recipient will need proof of identity in order to collect the funds. When transferring any funds make it absolutely clear on the forms what the funds are for particularly if the money is for building property as it might be the only proof of payment that you have.

Translations – there are no fully authorised translators operating in Luxor. Translation services are generally offered by Tour Guides or by friends with some English who have no legal knowledge of various terms that might be used. Be very wary. There are certified translators in Cairo and documents can be sent to them by fax. The service is quick and efficient and totally cost effective because once you have signed the papers it is too late to put things right. Property scams, business deals and many other transactions that involve legal documents offer open house to fraud if they are not properly checked. All papers that are approved in the court house, however small, have to be signed as being accurately translated by a tour guide/translator if foreigners are involved. This is an acceptable solution for inconsequential things but more care is needed for contracts that involve large sums of money. Caveat Emptor – Buyer Beware. Be careful rather than sorry.

Transvestites – each season there are several transvestite visitors in Luxor and they invoke a lot of giggling and whispering among the waiters that serve them in the coffee shops. There is amusement rather than aggression. I have only ever seen one Egyptian transvestite and he caused the same degree of amusement and interest among the local women who saw him.

Triad – (group of three) much of Egypt's ancient religions were based on Triads which could have set the scene for later acceptance of the triad of Christianity. Thebes had two important triads as part of its culture, Amun, Mut and Khonsu and then Isis, Osiris and Horus. There are temples and chapels to all of them in Luxor. Isis, Osiris and Horus best fit the later Coptic triad of Jesus, Mary and Joseph as, according to one version of the Osiris myth, Horus like Jesus sprang from a virgin birth as Osiris's penis had been eaten by the fishes. However, according to the lurid reliefs in the Ptolemaic temple at Dendera, Horus was conceived when Isis mounted Osiris's well-endowed corpse.

Tuk-tuks – are basically motorbikes with an open or covered cart attached to the back and are usually associated with transporting people in Asian countries but they have recently been introduced in Egypt. On the East Bank they are used as delivery vehicles being piled high with impossible loads but on the West Bank they are used for ferrying people about as well as materials and whole groups of workmen can be seen perched in the back. They are not as yet used for transporting people in town.

Turtle Doves – are of the pigeon family but are smaller and more delicate in shape and colour. They are basically a greyish brown with pink overtones and are common on both sides of the river. Also to be seen are collared doves and laughing doves which are also of a pinkish colour.

Tutankhamun – is perhaps Luxor's most famous Pharaoh although he was insignificant in his own time. He owes his fame to the discovery of his intact tomb in the Valley of the Kings. The tomb is disappointingly small and expensive to visit (an extra 100 LE) but is currently open to the public (although possibly for not much longer). His treasures are on display in the Egyptian Museum in Cairo. He was probably the son of Akhenaten and came to the throne of Egypt at an early age. On the death of his father he turned away from monotheism and the worship of Aten and restored Amun as Thebes's primary deity. He died an early and mysterious death that has fascinated archaeologists for decades. However, an earlier theory that he was murdered was disproved by recent tests on his mummy and possible causes now seem to be either blood-poisoning as a result of an infected wound, or congenital epilepsy. He was married to his half-sister Ankhesenamun but died without an heir.

Tutankhamun's Tomb – (KV62) was discovered in 1922 by Howard Carter in an excavation that was financed by Lord Carnarvon. The tomb was largely intact (it had been entered but the robbers did not reach the burial chamber) and it was full of "wonderful things". The artefacts from the tomb are the main attraction at Cairo Museum but his mummy still lies inside the tomb although it was recently removed for scanning. To visit the tomb, an extra ticket needs to be bought from the ticket office (100 LE).

Tutmosis III – was either the 5th or 6th Pharaoh of the 18th dynasty depending on how you view his somewhat chequered succession. He was the legitimate heir of his father Tutmosis II but was only a child when his father died so his step-mother Hatshepsut (who was also his aunt) ruled as Regent. Seven years into this arrangement, Hatshepsut assumed the role of sole ruler and Tutmosis, probably much to his chagrin, was side-lined. However, as it was common in some civilisations for rulers to dispose of their rivals he was perhaps lucky to survive. It was another 15 years before, on the death of Hatshepsut, he became Pharaoh in his own right. He exacted his revenge on his step-mother by ordering the destruction of many of her monuments. The 'holy' obelisks at Karnak were walled up, which fortunately acted to protect them rather than destroy them. He was an ambitious man and extended Egypt's borders to the north-east and into Nubia in the south and is buried in tomb KV34 which is high in the cliffs of the Valley of the Kings. You have to climb up a series to ladders to get there but it is worth the effort. The tomb is not as brightly decorated as some of the tombs on the Valley floor but it is interesting. However, it is not open to the public at the time of writing. (See Hatshepsut).

Twinky's – is Luxor's famous cake shop and is near the station end of Manshia Street. The branded cakes sold in the supermarkets under that name are popular imports but are no longer produced. The cakes from Twinky's shop can be delicious but sometimes have a tendency to be a bit dry. However, their biscuits and their biscuit based tarts are delicious.

Twinky Street – is so called because of the cake shop. Its actual name is Manshia Street.

Seti I Wearing the Uraeus

U

Upper Egypt - Utilities

Upper Egypt – is so called because it is in the upper reaches of the Nile although when you look at a map it is to the south and appears below the delta area. The Upper and Lower countries were unified by King Narmer around 3000 BCE. The crown of Upper Egypt was white and later Pharaohs are shown wearing the double crown, a combination of the red crown of Lower Egypt with the white crown of Upper Egypt.

Uraeus – is a cobra in its striking form. The cobra had a protective role for Egyptian royalty and its upright form was used to bestow divine authority on the wearer. It is seen on the headdresses of many Pharaohs including the magnificent mask of Tutankhamun held in Cairo Museum. The Uraeus is also associated with Isis as she is thought to have made the first cobra and used one to bite Ra and trick him into revealing his real name so that she could restore Osiris.

Urine – your urine should be clear and copious. If it is dark brown and sludgy then you are severely dehydrated. It is convenient in Luxor's heat not to have to visit a toilet for many hours at a time but it is not good for your kidneys. Wherever you go, take water with you. It is a common sight, and perfectly acceptable, for Egyptian men to urinate discretely by the roadside so do not be shocked if you witness this.

Utensils – if you need cooking utensils or household items, there are several all-purpose shops in the souk and around Luxor including Abu El Nakaar and Maraad Sherif in Television Street.

Utilities – the offices for the water and electricity companies can be found in Khaled Ibn el Walid Street and the offices of Egypt Telecom are in Temple Karnak Street.. The main post office is in Station Street. On the west bank the telephone office is close to the cemetery in the El Genena area of Qurna and the postal sorting office is at Seul.

Fruit and Vegetables in the Market

V

Vaccinations – Vultures

Vaccinations – there is no real need for special vaccinations before visiting Luxor, the ones you have had as protection in a home country such as measles, polio and tetanus will normally be all that you need. It could be useful to have a typhoid, smallpox and Hepatitis A vaccinations though if travelling about in remote areas. Egypt is not in the meningitis or malaria belts.

Valley of the Kings – is a canyon that winds its way through the Theban hills and is the final resting place of many of Egypt's New Kingdom Pharaohs; the most famous of which are Tutankhamun and Ramses the Great. The tomb of Ramses is not open to the public as it is in too great a state of decay but the tomb of Tutankhamun can be visited. A ticket bought at the entrance allows the bearer to visit any three of the open tombs except for the tombs of Tutankhamun and Ramses VI, which require extra tickets. To preserve the decorations in the tombs, they are closed regularly on a rotation basis so it is difficult to give a list of which ones are available to visit at any given time. Excavations in the Valley are on-going and discoveries are still being made but the main excavation is still on KV5 – the tomb of the sons of Ramses II.

Valley of the Monkeys – is the alternative name of the Western Valley which is a spur of the Valley of the Kings and contains the tomb of Ay which is open to the public. It also contains the tomb of Amenhotep III which is undergoing restoration but is not open to the public. There are no actual monkeys in the Valley and its name is derived from the paintings on the walls of Ay's tomb.

Valley of the Queens – is at the opposite end of the Theban Hills to the Valley of the Kings and holds the tombs of royal Princes as well as royal Wives. There are 78 tombs in the valley but only three are open to the public. The tomb of Nefertari, which is one of the most spectacular tombs in the Necropolis, has been closed to the public for several years. The open tombs are of Prince Amunherkhepshef, Prince Khaemwaset and Queen Tyti.

Vegetables – fresh vegetables are available in the supermarkets as well as the general markets but supermarket vegetables tend to be far more expensive without having any extra quality. In Upper Egypt the vegetables taste wonderful and come in all shapes and sizes. Some, such as cabbages and cauliflowers, are huge. The carrots are sweet and tender and the salad vegetables taste as they really should taste and not like nondescript clones available in European supermarkets.

Veils – the face veil worn by Egyptian women is called a Niqab. Few women in Luxor wear them but there has been a small increase in recent years.

Vermin – like all densely populated places, Luxor has more than its fair share of mammal and insect vermin such as rats and cockroaches. Beware of bed bugs in very cheap hotels. Rat traps can be bought in the souk. 'Raid' and other insecticides are easy to find and are very effective against cockroaches.

Viagra – is available over the counter in most pharmacies but care has to be taken as some have been found to be fake - containing Paracetamol rather than the real ingredients. Cialis is an alternative.

Villas – in Luxor villas are seldom actual houses as they are simply two flats (or more) one above the other in a detached building with a small garden. There are some single occupancy houses to be found but these have usually been built for individuals rather than for the tourist trade.

Visas – for Egypt are obtainable on arrival at Luxor Airport and cost $15 at the time of writing. They are valid for 1 month and if you intend staying longer you will need to apply for an extension (a 2 week period of grace is added to the basic 1 month visa but thereafter you may be refused exit if you turn up at the airport without having obtained an extension). They can be paid for in any currency. Take care when buying your visa as often there is a rip-off with prices of around £20 per person being quoted. Visa renewal can be obtained from the passport office in Khaled Ibn el Walid Street but the maximum extension given at present (2013) is six months.

Vomiting – if you find yourself vomiting because of a tummy upset, regardless of what medicine you take for it, remember to drink copious amounts of water or you will become dehydrated very quickly.

Vultures – 'Pharaoh's chickens' appear prominently in ancient Egyptian art and are seen on necklaces, headdresses and carved into door lintels in the temples. They, along with the ibis, were considered sacred. Vultures were widespread throughout Egypt but have declined rapidly although they can sometimes be seen soaring on the thermals. The goddess Maat is often shown with the wings of a white vulture.

A Saqiya Water Wheel

W
Wadi – Wudu

Wadi – is Arabic for 'valley' but the term is also applied to dry riverbeds. 'Wadi biban el Malouk' is the 'Valley of the Kings'.

Waiters – waiters are extremely poorly paid in Luxor and are dependent on tips. Many of them have a Government job in the mornings and work late into the night in the restaurants and coffee shops. Bear this in mind when leaving a tip. Not many of them speak English so be patient if your order is misunderstood.

Walking – so long as you take precautions with your belongings, walking around Luxor and the west bank necropolis is perfectly safe. There are some interesting walks around the town but the most spectacular is the west bank walk that leads you over the hill from the Valley of the Kings to the Temple of Hatshepsut although there have been reports of this walk now being prohibited from the Valley of the Kings side. There is another spectacular but long walk from the Carter House to the Temple of Thoth above the Western Valley. Also a favourite is to walk up the hill from the Valley of the Queens to the Meretseger shrine at the top and then over to the other side and down the steps to Deir el Medina.

Wallahi – means 'I swear to God' and Egyptians often use it many times in one sentence. You will hear it crop up in almost all conversations even those that are conducted in English.

Wardens – when the British Honorary Consul in Luxor had to leave his post after a change in Egyptian law, the Embassy proposed setting up a volunteer warden system to advise UK expats of what to do if and when there is a crisis. Steps have been taken to organise the warden system but it is still to be finalised.

Waset – is the ancient Egyptian name for Luxor.

Water – ('mayya') tap water is very heavily chlorinated and many expats are accustomed to it but it is not recommended for visitors. Mineral water is available in most shops at around 2 LE or 3 LE per litre (much higher in the hotels). Remember to drink much more than you would at home or else you will become dehydrated.

Water-Wheels – Water needs to be regularly raised from the canals to fill the irrigation channels that bring water to crops. There are few water wheels in use now as most water is raised by mechanical pumps. There were many different ways of raising the water but the most common was the 'shadouf' which is a levered pole with a bucket or jar on one end and a counterweight on the other that allowed a dipped bucket to be raised and swung without a great deal of effort. Actual wheels ('saqiyas') are rarely used, but their remains can be seen throughout the West Bank. There is a working version, drawn by oxen at Saqiya, an agricultural museum and park south of Luxor.

Weather – although Luxor is a desert area it has distinct seasons. There is an average of only 1 mm of rain a year and temperatures can be well above 40C in the summer. However, every few years there is torrential rain which can lead to devastating floods, taking lives and destroying mud brick houses. Although humidity should be very low, evaporation from Lake Nasser can cause uncomfortable humidity especially in spring. Also in spring, there are dust storms as the 'Khamseen' winds blow in from the Sahara. In winter, nights can be cold and you may need a jacket. Remember that at this latitude the sun is far stronger than it is in European resorts.

Weddings – wedding celebrations take place over three days and are noisy affairs. The night of the first day is a men-only affair with music and lots of sitting about; the second night is the main celebration. First there is a visit to the photographer, accompanied by a troupe of drummers, which is followed by a procession of cars and motorbikes madly rushing around the town to proclaim the wedding. After that the couple gather in their village street and are seated on a dais to watch dancing and listen to music. Richer couples will entertain their guests in a hotel but most will use their home and the street outside or a piece of clear land in the village. At some time during the evening the bride's gold will be presented to her then the couple will leave to consummate the marriage. The next morning friends and relatives will visit the couple's new home to view the presents. This is when, by tradition, the blood stained sheet would be displayed but this is no longer done. There is no religious service or contract signing involved in the actual 'wedding' as the marriage could have taken place quite some time before. The wedding is a declaration that the couple now have somewhere to live, even if it is only a small room in the groom's mother's house, and that the marriage will be consummated.

Wedjet Eye – is a stylised eye complete with its brow often referred to as the 'eye of Horus'. Horus lost an eye to Seth in their fearsome battle but Thoth healed it and returned it to him whole. They were used as amulets for protection and can be found as bracelets and necklaces for personal wear as well as being found in tombs and on coffins.

Wells – although most families, even those in the outer villages have access to piped water even if it is only from a stand-pipe in the street, there are still areas dependent on water drawn up from wells. In 'richer' households this will be done with a pump but in many places water is still raised by hand-turning a winch system that lifts a bucket.

West Bank – life on the west bank of the Nile differs greatly from life on the eastern side of the river. The pace is slower, traffic is infinitely lighter and there is a rural atmosphere. There are few shops but there are some attractive hotels and most of the antiquities are in the necropolis on this side of the river. The area is mainly referred to as Qurna but is actually a series of villages that more or less run into each other. It is reached either by ferry, motor boat or via the bridge which lies 10 km south of Luxor.

Western Valley – the Western Valley is also known as the Valley of the Monkeys and runs off the Valley of the Kings. It is a wonderful lonely place reminiscent of what the Valley of the

Kings would have been like thousands of years ago. There are several tombs in the valley but only the tomb of Ay, who was Tutankhamun's Prime Minister, is open to the public. (See Valley of the Monkeys.)

Wi-Fi – in Luxor Wi-Fi connections are usually through Vodafone or Etisalat dongles obtained from any of the mobile telephone shops. The service is becoming cheaper and more reliable as, with the rising sales of smartphones, more people are using them in preference to ADSL. In-house Wi-Fi through a land-line router is also available. McDonald's and Snacktime offer a free service so you can answer your emails while having a cup of coffee in air-conditioned surroundings.

Wills – to be legal in Egypt a will has to be written in Arabic. You can leave instructions on what is to happen to your remains with your embassy but Egyptian law will cover the distribution of your immoveable assets such as any real estate. Egyptian law (in the absence of a will) is very different from European law and professional advice should be sought when drawing up the will. So, if you have property in Luxor then make sure that you have a will in Arabic stating who is to inherit your effects/estate.

Wines - there are more than 15 different wines available in Luxor with Obelisk, Omar Khayyam and Sheherazade being the most popular. They can be bought from the wine shops in the souk and from the Duty Free shops. JJ's in Karnak has the widest range offered by a restaurant but several other restaurants including The Lantern also have an alcohol license and a wine list.

Winter Palace – is Luxor's most famous hotel and is now managed by the Sofitel Group. It was built in 1886 on the eastern bank of the Nile to provide appropriate accommodation for the rich and famous that came to Egypt with Thomas Cook. It has a magnificent façade and a superb rear garden.

Work Permits – it is easy for tourists to become obsessed with Egypt and want to stay after their holiday is finished. Extensions to visas which state that work is not allowed are not hard to get but work permits are very hard to obtain. They must be applied for by the employer and are job specific. All foreigners applying for work permits have to undergo a mandatory AIDS test.

Workers' Village – Deir el Medina (Monastery of the Town) is the village where the workers (quarrymen, sculptors, stonecutters, painters etc.) who dug and decorated the tombs of the Pharaohs lived. It was originally called 'Set Maat' – The Place of Truth and was only important during the New Kingdom era as it was abandoned when the Pharaohs moved north. There is a small but atmospheric Ptolemaic temple to Hathor there and three tombs are usually open to the public – (Pashedu, Sennedjem and Inherkau – but the tomb of Inherkau is presently closed.) The tomb of Irynefer, which is close to the temple, has recently been opened. All these tombs are worth visiting. Tickets are necessary and can be bought at the ticket office; a separate ticket is required for Pashedu's tomb. Excavation of the area has revealed a treasure-trove of ostraca which are notelets written on pottery shards. These have given a great insight into the lives of ordinary Egyptian people.

Writers – the late Naquib Mafouz is the most famous Egyptian writer and was awarded the Nobel Prize for Literature in 1988. He wrote 38 novels; among which was the Cairo Trilogy. The most well-known contemporary Egyptian writer is Adhaf Soueif (The Map of Love) who is a novelist and political commentator. Wilbur Smith (River God Series), Barbara Erskine (Whispers in the Sand), Agatha Christie (Death on the Nile), Elizabeth Peters (Amelia Peabody Series), the late Paul Sussman (Last Secret of the Temple) and many more have all written best-selling novels about Egypt; a subject which continues to fascinate readers. A vast number of eminent Egyptologists have written about Egyptian history among which Kent Weeks is perhaps the most notable when discussing Luxor. (See Recommended Reading.)

Wudu - is the ritual washing of the face, feet, hands and arms that Muslims complete before praying.

X

X - No entries

Y

Yalla – Youth Hostel

Yalla – is commonly used to say 'come on 'or 'let's get going'.

Yani – is a word that crops up in most conversations. It is the Arabic equivalent of 'er' or 'um'.

Yes – (aywa) if someone answers a question with a single 'yes' in English then it indicates understanding of your question but if the answer is a double 'Yes yes' then you have probably not been understood.

Yesterday – is 'embara' in Arabic.

Youth Hostel - there is an extremely large Youth Hostel at El Tod which is about 20 km south of Luxor.

Z

Zakat - Zoo

Zakat – is the annual payment made by Muslim families to the mosque for redistribution as alms for the poor which is one of the five pillars of Islam.

Zebadi – if you want yoghurt with your breakfast then ask for 'zebadi'

Zebda – if you want butter with your bread or toast then ask for 'zebda.'

Zoo – there is a small zoo which has caused great concern to animal welfare groups in the children's playground site in Television Street. ACE and Brook are making regular visits now to ensure the safe keeping of the animals some of which have been removed.

Queen Hatshepsut

Reading List

Gods and Myths of Ancient Egypt - Robert A. Armour – American University in Cairo Press (2010)

The Tomb-Builders of the Pharoahs - Morris Bierbrier – American University in Cairo Press – 1993

Carnarvon and Carter – Lady Fiona Carnarvon – Highclere Enterprises (2007)

The Complete Pharaohs - Peter A. Clayton – American University in Cairo Press (2006)

Mummies Myth and Magic - Christine El Mahdy – Thames & Hudson (1991)

The Tombs of the Nobles at Luxor - Lise Manniche - American University in Cairo (1988)

Temples, Tombs and Hieroglyphs - Barbara Mertz – William Morrow (2009)

The Private Lives of the Pharaohs - Joyce Tyldesley – TV Books (2001)

The Illustrated Guide to Luxor - Kent R. Weeks – American University in Cairo Press (2005)

The Valley of the Kings – A Site Management Handbook – Kent Weeks and Nigel Hetherington – American University in Cairo Press (2013)

Acknowledgements

I would like to thank Stan Kurowski for his patience and for freely giving his time to edit and add photographs to this Lexicon. A multitude of thanks are offered to Christian Miller whose edits, recommendations and chastisements were invaluable in keeping this book on course and reining in my excessive enthusiasm. Bernie Flingers, Doc Venner, Nita Tavlin, Mary Crowther and Mick Tindale are thanked for their advice and support as the book progressed and Sue Park is thanked for proof reading the script. Special thanks are due to Nagar Khalifa for offering extra local knowledge and for answering my endless questions.

All proceeds from the sale of this book are being donated to Little Stars - Luxor Children's Trust for the care and education of Luxor's most deprived children and everyone gave their help willingly and freely.

Biographies

Connie Tindale - author

Connie Tindale lived in a small village on the west bank of the Nile for five years and has lived in the east bank for the last ten years. She is the chairman of a local children's charity and has a long-term interest in Egypt's history and its culture. She can be contacted on Admin@Amunpublishing.com

Stan Kurowski – editor

Stan Kurowski lives on the West Bank of the Nile at Luxor. He is deeply interested in Egyptian history and archaeology and is a keen photographer. He also designs websites for local businesses. Stan can be contacted on Stan@EternalEgypt.co.uk

Christian Miller – editor

Chris Miller has lived in Hurghada for seven years and is a frequent visitor to Luxor where he occasionally accompanies visitors to the historic sites. He has had a lifelong interest in Egypt and its heritage and is also an avid naturalist.

Notes

4562860R00117

Printed in Great Britain
by Amazon.co.uk, Ltd.,
Marston Gate.